Northern Flights

Northern Flights

*Tracking the Birds and Birders
of Michigan's Upper Peninsula*

SHERYL DE VORE

Illustrations by Denis Kania
With a Foreword by Dr. Eldon Greij

Mountain Press Publishing Company
Missoula, Montana
1999

Library of Congress Cataloging-in-Publication Data

De Vore, Sheryl.
    Northern flights : tracking the birds and birders of Michigan's
Upper Peninsula / Sheryl De Vore ; illustrated by Denis
Kania : with a foreword by Eldon Greij.
        p   cm.
    Includes bibliographical references (p.   ) and index.
    ISBN 0-87842-400-8 (alk. paper)
    1. Birds—Michigan—Upper Peninsula.   2. Bird watching—
Michigan—Upper Peninsula.   I. Title.
QL684.M5D475   1999
598'.09774'9—dc21   99-29655
                                                              CIP

Printed in the United States of America

Mountain Press Publishing Company
P.O. Box 2399 • Missoula, Montana 59806
406-728-1900

For my father, Raymond Osterman,
who taught me to embark on life's journeys
with joie de vivre, *bravery, and humility.*

Michigan's Upper Peninsula

ONTARIO

Sault Ste. Marie

LAKE HURON

Michigan's Lower Peninsula

LAKE MICHIGAN

LAKE SUPERIOR

Whitefish Point Bird Observatory

Paradise

Whitefish Bay

Whitefish Point

Hiawatha National Forest

Lake Superior State Forest

Seney NWR

Pictured Rocks NL

Hiawatha National Forest

Yellow Dog Plains

Estivant Pines Nature Sanctuary

Copper Harbor

Keweenaw Bay

Houghton

HURON MOUNTAINS

Keweenaw Peninsula

Escanaba

Norway

Sylvania Wilderness Area

Ottawa National Forest

Ontonagon

Watersmeet

Lake Gogebic

Porcupine Mtns.

Trap Hills

WISCONSIN

Isle Royale National Park (48 miles from UP mainland)

N

Contents

Foreword

B IRDS, LIKE ALL ANIMALS, are products of their environment and can best be appreciated in the context of the habitats in which they live. This book, following that principle, describes a rugged, little-known wilderness and some of the birds that claim it as home.

Sheryl De Vore is a writer with a profound understanding of the natural world as well as an abiding commitment to birds. In this book, she brings Michigan's spectacular Upper Peninsula to life, taking the reader on a detailed, time-warp journey into its history and providing us with fascinating essays about some of the intriguing birds that live there, with insightful anecdotes and stories from people who study them. Each chapter is a plea to protect this rare habitat so these birds, many rare or in jeopardy, can continue to thrive.

Michigan, a nature lover's dream, took an eternity to create. Half a million years ago, glaciers of immense proportions advanced like giant tongues, pushing aside everything in their way. Finally, temperatures rose and the massive glaciers retreated, having scoured the rock beneath them and gouged great depressions that would fill with water and become the Great Lakes.

Nothing so dominates a map of the United States as these lakes that create the mitten-like shape of Michigan. With its white sand dunes, sheer cliffs, and forests, the coasts of Michigan offer a beauty unique to our continent.

Within the confines of Michigan's two great peninsulas, one now tamed and the other still wild, is an amazing assortment of birds. It is the Upper Peninsula—the wild one—that Sheryl shows us.

Sheryl takes us to loon country, introducing us to a unique team of researchers. We learn of the many holes in our knowledge of loons. Do loons really mate for life? Why do some loons change mates in the middle of the breeding season? And why are dead loons being found with unusually high levels of mercury in their systems?

We also travel to Whitefish Point, arguably the best birding site in the UP. Located in the northeastern corner, the Point extends into Lake Superior as a beacon to migrating birds that pass over in tremendous numbers. Sheryl introduces us to a hawk counter who shares parts of her diary in which she recorded frigid spring days on the lonely, wind-swept Point. We meet researchers studying sharp-shinned hawks in a makeshift wooden banding shack. Also working at Whitefish are the gluttons-for-punishment owl banders, who begin their work in April, a spring month in some southerly climes but a midwinter month at the Point. We accompany Sheryl and the banding crews, checking mist nets from dusk to dawn.

Sheryl next brings us to a wet sedge meadow in the middle of the UP to find the yellow rail, one of the most sought-after species on the continent. The breeding habitat of the rail needs protection if this bird, which is listed as threatened in Michigan, is to survive.

The UP also harbors three spectacular species of grouse. Sheryl shows us how one man, devoted to the sharp-tailed grouse for twenty-five years, is fighting to save them, and appears to be winning the cause. It is the spruce grouse, however, that claims the attention of most UP birders. Sheryl leaves us with a yearning to find these birds that perform intricate courtship dances each spring.

We also go with Sheryl to the western UP and the Porcupine Mountains to learn how the peregrine falcon is being brought back from the brink of extinction. And we journey with her on census routes as researchers study neotropical migrants that breed or pass through the UP.

If you are planning a trip to the beckoning wilderness of Michigan's UP, you can observe firsthand the beauty and experiences Sheryl describes. In the meantime, enjoy the journey she has written for you. May your interest in nature be enhanced by this book, and may we all work to ensure that birds continue their northern flights through the UP.

Dr. Eldon Greij
Founding editor of *Birder's World*

Preface

SEVEN YEARS AGO, during a week when I was facing the unkind part of living, I discovered a place where murky bogs cleansed my soul and green curtains of light illuminated a darkened spirit. On an April day at dusk, a lone long-eared owl flew over Whitefish Bay in Michigan's Upper Peninsula across the aurora borealis, taking some of life's harshness with it. I have never forgotten that moment—and I was compelled to return again and again.

On my second trip, I spent time with Rick Baetsen, a man who has devoted his life to protecting habitat in the UP.

On my way home along a winding road through forests and marshy openings, I heard a sound that beckoned me to stay. *OOOGA LUNK—OOGA LUNK.* An American bittern. Extending its neck to look like just another marsh plant, the bittern bellowed its old pumplike call from the Labrador tea. It was precisely at that moment I decided to write a book about the UP, not only about the unique birds that live there, but also about the people I had met who live there and are working to save the birds. The bittern represents the steadfast nature of the men and women who work quietly behind the scenes in marshes, woods, forests, and grasslands to protect wild avian creatures.

Not many know about the unique lives they lead; their stories are told here.

It took eight years to write this book. It has been a personal journey in which I have learned revealing things about myself that I hope will make me a better human being. I have also met some of the most wonderful human beings on Earth, who have helped me mold what you are now reading.

I must thank them all now, as well as the important people in my life who have supported me through this adventure. Karl DeVore spent much of his vacation time over the past four years in the UP driving scrub-board roads surrounded by marshes and bogs. He climbed rugged cliffs and sat in a cold, damp blind at 4 A.M. to wait for sharp-tailed grouse. He drove through Lake Superior fog at 2 A.M., fifty miles back to our cabin after a strenuous birding excursion. (But don't worry. He had a wonderful time!)

From the very start, my twin sister, Laurel Ann Kaiser, encouraged me to keep working on this book. She is my most supportive friend and a wonderful companion.

My dear friend Mary Katharine Parks Workinger also never faltered in her faith in me. A skillful editor, she knew just the right things to say to help bring this book to life. I also thank Chuck Hutchcraft, a fellow Zen believer, confidant, editor, and writer. His interest in my writing and personal growth has meant more than he knows. Mountain Press editor Kathleen Ort's suggestions for improvement really helped make this work sing. I thank her and the rest of the editorial staff.

The following people have read portions of this book, offering wisdom, different points of view, and needed corrections. To them I owe many, many thanks, as well as sincere apologies for any errors that may have gone uncorrected. These are also the people who want to protect the UP and the birds that live there. You will meet many of them in this book.

One of them is Rick Baetsen, a genuine conservationist who, with his wife, Bonnie, is teaching his three children important lessons in life: how to recognize the identity of Michigan's butterflies, how to camp in the north woods, and how to find a dancing sharp-tailed grouse. Rick is a true friend and an inspiration.

Rick also introduced me to two extraordinary people, Joe and Barb Rogers. They spent a week helping me experience the UP wilderness in a way I never had before. Joe and Barb taught me how to climb cliffs and kayak on Lake Superior.

Special thanks also go to David Evers, whom I met eight years ago when he was the director of Whitefish Point Bird Observatory. Since then, I have followed his career as he studied loons and created a research group dedicated to preserving these and other creatures. Pete Reaman, one of Dave's partners, has also been helpful and encouraging. Pete called me several years ago on a bleak, wintery Saturday night to ask how he could help with the book, and introduced me to Richard Urbanek at Seney National Wildlife Refuge. Even after rising at 4:30 A.M. to do songbird counts, Richard remained awake until well past midnight to take me to search for yellow rails. Denis Kania, who illustrated this book, also deserves my gratitude for his insightful and well-crafted work.

One person dedicated to education and ornithology must also be mentioned: Eldon Greij, the founder of *Birder's World,* who wrote this book's foreword and has contributed much to the birding community. Gratitude also goes to my friend and birding companion Renee Baade, who accompanied me to the UP for a week while I researched the book.

Special thanks also go to Susan Andres, Robert Doepker, Jim Granlund, Richard and Brenda Keith, Brian Kenner, Walter Johansen, Mike Mossman, Robert Sprague, Mary Teesdale, John Urbain, and Russell Utych, who read the book for accuracy and many of whom continue to help the birds in the UP. Mary Hennen of the Chicago Academy of Sciences also helped fine-tune the scientific aspects of several chapters.

Many others are also out there working for the birds of Michigan's Upper Peninsula. They are not named in this book, not because they do not deserve it, but because there are so many and I haven't met them all yet. These people quietly and determinedly work to protect not just the birds, but also the UP ecosystem. This book is for them.

Northern Flights

MID-JANUARY, DUSK. A ravine along Sugar Island near Sault Ste. Marie in the easternmost part of Michigan's Upper Peninsula. A local wanderer, wearing thick, heavy boots and layered clothing pauses to rest on his way back to civilization. He blows warm steam on cold, cupped hands, then looks to a pine tree atop which is poised a two-foot-tall owl with ringed facial disks and clear, yellow eyes. A great gray owl. Some wonder if this large, North American owl breeds in the UP, its southernmost range. But this day, in winter's darkest time, the owl is looking only for food. It lifts silent wings and flies out into a forest clearing, leaving a memory of its image behind.

Late April, late afternoon. Spruces and pines provide an energizing scent to a traveler on the road to Whitefish Point Bird Observatory fifty miles west of Sault Ste. Marie. Patches of snow, crusty and crystalline from long bouts of below-freezing temperatures, remain. Unpolluted forty-five-degree air fills the lungs, startling with its raw freshness.

Pe-TEE Pe-TEE.

A broad-winged hawk calls, then flies into the pines.

Like every other creature and plant here, the trees are poised between winter and spring. The lengthening days, coupled with warm spells that thaw ice into needed moisture, will trigger renewal.

Some open water beyond a damp field of rusty-hued Labrador tea harbors several ring-necked ducks. A male wears his nuptial plumage: glossy black breast, neck, head, and back with a grayish white body. He will soon pursue the drabber, less-conspicuous females. For now, he gives a one-pitched, hollow alarm call and steals into the shadows, holding his crested head upright.

Late May, 10 A.M. Somewhere along the rocky Lake Superior shoreline, a male and female peregrine falcon choose a cliff on which to nest.

EEEEEEEE.

The female screams from her nest site, nothing more than a small depression at the cliff's edge. Her mate returns with a meal clutched in his talons. She flies to meet him, grabbing the prey in the air as he drops it to her.

Meanwhile, near an old Coast Guard station in the northeastern UP, dawn brings fog with humid air along Lake Superior's shoreline. White lady's slippers stick like warm, melting marshmallows on the spongy bog. A distant rattle signals the presence of sandhill cranes. Five of these long-legged creatures fly in a tight constellation. Their wings pound the air as they sail above the ground, then disappear into a marsh.

Quick-three-beers.

An olive-sided flycatcher finds a barren tree on which to perch and challenge another to its territorial hold.

In the mist, a loon wails.

One hundred miles away in Norway, Michigan, near the southwestern edge of the UP, blackburnian warblers with throats the orange of cheddar cheese whisper their breeding songs among eastern hemlocks, basswood, and other deciduous and coniferous trees. Black-throated green warblers sing *Zoo Zee Zoo Zoo Zee* from the treetops while the ground-nesting ovenbird chants an incessant *Teacher Teacher.*

June 20, midnight. The longest day of the year. Seney National Wildlife Refuge in the central UP. Common snipes winnow in the hot air, their tail feathers whistling as they plunge to romance their mates in the twilight. Marsh wrens and sedge wrens chatter from grasses perspiring with evening dew.

Tick Tick Ticky Tick.

The rare yellow rail, ensconced among the sedges, remains unseen as it vigorously announces its intentions with its percussive mating call.

Early October, 8 A.M. Sugar maples shine yellow and red through the leaves of eastern hemlocks in the Porcupine Mountains in the western UP. Tall black spruces narrow at their peaks. The last trickle of migrating songbirds lingers here. Exhausted from summer breeding, these birds no longer sing, but chip softly as they snatch the last of the insects before flying south for winter. Loons, grebes, ducks, and shorebirds fly along the Lake Superior shoreline across the northern expanse of the UP, wending their way to their winter homes.

The following chapters tell the stories of the birds of Michigan's Upper Peninsula, their natural history, and their struggle to endure in an ecosystem created by geological forces thousands of years ago. Here also are the stories of researchers who find refuge and purpose in an uncommon way of life, working with the avian creatures of northern Michigan.

Many more volunteer and paid researchers than described here work with the avian creatures of the UP. Some come never to return again. Others return to sate a yearning. Still others remain here their entire lives. All have been irrevocably changed by their experiences as they work to improve the health of an ecosystem and its ability to provide habitat for some of the rarest birds in North America.

Cape May Warbler

Paradise Unfolds

BEFORE LAKE SUPERIOR was even a glimmer in North America's geological history—long before the glaciers came; before loons, songbirds, cranes, owls, hawks, rails, and grouse began raising young; and before humans entered the evolving ecosystem—the story of Michigan's Upper Peninsula began to unfold.

Continental drift, the creation and destruction of mountains, climate changes, and a series of ice ages, particularly the last one, paved the way for the development of the fens, lakes, bogs, waterfalls, boreal and mixed deciduous forests, cliffs, and hillsides, all of which provide habitat for an astounding variety of plants and animals living in the wilderness people call the UP. Some 2 to 3 billion years ago, the area that now includes the five Great Lakes belonged to a growing continent bounded by shallow seas and offshore volcanic islands. Geologically, this area was alive. Mobile plates moving over the earth's molten interior alternately drifted apart and together, colliding or sliding atop one another and creating mountains and volcanoes.

The intense pressure and heat of the continental collisions created metamorphic rock such as crystalline schists and gneisses. Lava flowed across the landscape, accumulating in thick layers that eventually cooled and sagged. The resulting depression became Lake Superior almost 1 billion years later. Wind and water whittled away the mountains and volcanoes, but the rocks created by this geological unrest became the bedrock for what is now Isle Royale National Park, the Porcupine Mountains and the Trap Hills in the western UP, and Pictured Rocks National Lakeshore at Lake Superior's southern shore. Some of the world's oldest exposed rocks crop out in the western UP, and some contain copper and other ores mined in recent years.

Half a million years ago, the earth's climate cooled, and a continental glacier, spreading across thousands of miles from a center near Hudson Bay in Canada, covered the entire state of Michigan. This glacier moved like a frozen amoeba with dips, peaks, and cracks on its surface, and with rivers of water flowing beneath it.

The ice brought rock particles from Canada—boulders, pebbles, and sand that scoured and scraped the landscape beneath the glacier. Ten or more advances of heavy ice, sometimes one-quarter mile thick, advanced, retreated, advanced, and retreated. As the last glacier chilling the upper half of North America retreated 12,000 to 15,000 years ago, a remarkable ecosystem emerged on what is now Michigan's Upper Peninsula. The ice melted sporadically, leaving behind mounds and ridges of till: randomly arranged mixtures of silt, clay, sand, gravel, and boulders. The glaciers scoured and polished the Porcupine and Huron Mountains in the western and scraped flat the land in the eastern UP. Rushing meltwater forged rivers, while retreating glaciers broke in stranded, detached chunks that melted beneath glacial debris to form depressions in the landscape called kettles. Some of these kettles became glacial lakes harboring the fish that ducks, eagles, and loons eat. Shallower kettles became bogs and wetlands where American bitterns, herons, and cranes feed on aquatic delicacies. In the flatter central and eastern UP, a mosaic of marshes and sedge meadows developed, some deep, others shallow, depending upon the lay of the land.

The repeated glacial advances and retreats sculpted the basins of the Great Lakes—perhaps the most prominent Ice Age features in North America. Lake Superior, the largest body of water produced by the glaciers, is 350 miles long, 150 miles wide, and 1,300 feet deep. It contains nearly 10 percent of the globe's fresh water and encompasses 2,726 miles of shoreline, about one-third of it along the northern edge of the UP. Lake Michigan separates the Upper Peninsula from the Lower Peninsula, with islands dotting the water between the two. The third Great Lake that defines this area as a peninsula is Lake Huron, at the UP's southeastern end.

Ten thousand to 12,000 years ago, a warming climate pushed the boreal and mixed forests north out of Michigan's Lower Peninsula,

Wisconsin, and northern Illinois; but areas of the Upper Peninsula, where the climate stayed cooler, became a transitional boreal forest zone, a connection to Michigan's northern neighbor, Canada. You can still contemplate what the Upper Peninsula, the Lower Peninsula, Wisconsin, and the northern one-third to one-half of Illinois looked like soon after the glaciers retreated some 15,000 years ago by wandering through the UP's boreal and hardwood forests and wetlands. These relic ecosystems remain in the UP, even after logging, mining, and water channelization disrupted them. While drier, warmer conditions in the Midwest some 8,000 years ago allowed the emergence of the great prairies, the climate remained cooler in the UP, leading to the development of four dominant tree communities: spruces and firs; maples, beeches, and birches; aspens and birches; and white, red, and jack pines. Growing within these tree communities are other hardwoods, such as oaks, and conifers, including the widely distributed but declining eastern hemlock.

The plants that grow in the cold and wet UP have adapted to thrive in this ecosystem. Different tree communities dominate depending on latitude, proximity to water, and soil type. Each community offers respite for various animals that also evolved here. In the bog ecosystem, for example, where acidic conditions make moisture less available, the leathery skin of the low-lying leatherleaf shrub helps it hold the water it needs to survive. In the coniferous forest ecosystem, conifers adapt to the cold and snow by dropping needles, not all at once as deciduous trees do in autumn, but slowly throughout the year. The ever-present clusters of needles help break the flow of wind across branches, reducing wind chill and evaporation. The needles' waxy coating also reduces water loss. An antifreeze-like chemical inside the needle helps protect against frost damage. The soft, thick layer of slowly decomposing needles on the forest floor and the highly flammable resin within these needles, create an ideal condition for fire, which is essential for regeneration in jack pine forests. Heat causes the pinecones to open and release their seeds. Rodents living in the thick layer of fallen conifer needles provide food to owls, accipiters, and other raptors that migrate through on their way to and from Canada across Lake Superior. Some species that live farther north in Canada, such as the great gray owl, may invade the UP during years of low food productivity in their normal living quarters.

The jack pine, spruce, and fir habitats attract a unique assemblage of animals that can glean food in ways that other species cannot. Boreal chickadees and red-breasted nuthatches deftly search for insect eggs and larvae hidden in the trees' bark. Porcupines eat the bark, while red squirrels, red crossbills, and white-winged crossbills extract seeds from pine and spruce cones for sustenance. The crossbill's highly evolved beak allows it to pry open cones that would defeat other foragers. While most songbirds feed insects to nestlings, red crossbills feed their young mostly pine seeds.

These plants and animals live on a peninsula whose outline on a map resembles a rabbit running west and poised between two Great Lakes, Superior to the north and Michigan to the south. The rabbit's ears are the Keweenaw Peninsula, where northern hardwoods, including sugar maples, grow along with spruce, fir, and other boreal forest species. The rabbit's head consists of the Porcupine Mountains, the Trap Hills, and hundreds of miles of cliffs with pines, northern hardwoods, and some deciduous wetlands. The rabbit's arched back is Pictured Rocks National Lakeshore, and south of there northern hardwoods and evergreens grow. Near the rabbit's stomach is the flatter Seney National Wildlife Refuge, with deciduous swamps and coniferous bogs extending eastward toward Whitefish Point, which hugs the bay of the same name. Here, thousands of loons, grebes, ducks, hawks, and songbirds pause in their fall and spring migrations. Of the 409 species of birds accepted by the Michigan Bird Records Committee, more than 300 have been documented migrating through, resting, or breeding near Whitefish Point Bird Observatory, a hump at the east end of the rabbit's back. At the rabbit's front and back feet in the south-central and eastern UP are mixed deciduous/coniferous forests that attract breeding and feeding songbirds that partake of the copious insect life climaxing in June and July. More than 181 bird species breed in the central part of the UP alone.

The first humans probably came to the UP about 14,000 years ago as the ice began to melt. Nomadic Ice Age hunters migrated from Asia. They lived among now-extinct mastodons, giant beavers, and two-ton sloths, which they hunted along the edges of the receding glaciers. One Native American people, the Ojibwa, settled in northern Ontario and Michigan's UP and thrived here until the 1800s.

The Ojibwa believed a mysterious power or spirit lived in all things. These robust, dark-complected people revered the large copper rocks they found and carried pieces of copper with them for good luck. They built canoes out of the copious birches growing in the north woods and wigwams out of tree bark and bulrushes in the wetlands. They hunted, fished, and trapped animals, plying the wetlands in their canoes. Though no historical accounts detail the numbers of wildlife present here for the Ojibwa to consume, one can imagine the thousands of migrating and breeding ducks and the grouse they hunted. They also harvested wild rice, cranberries, and blueberries that grew in the bogs.

In winter, the Ojibwa told stories about the animal manitous, sacred creatures that held together the land upon which they lived. The Great Turtle created Earth and now carries it upon his back. The Great Fisher sang and danced to keep the lakeshore from disintegrating. Beavers created the rapids. Spawning whitefish harbored the singing spirits of ancient Ojibwa women.

European settlers came in the 1600s, sometimes living peacefully with the Ojibwa, other times not. In the end, they took the Native Americans' land but kept some of the names given to it—among them Keweenaw Peninsula, Tahquamenon Falls, and Lake Gogebic. In 1848, according to legend, an English gentleman found a six-ton mass of copper in the western UP that he said came from an ancient mining operation. His declaration brought others to search for the ancient copper mines of the western UP, where they hoped to make their fortunes. Some of them cut the forests and drained marshes for farmland. In the early 1900s, lumberjacks arrived to harvest red and white pines—not for use in the UP, which was still a great, unpopulated wilderness, but to be shipped via channelized rivers and the Great Lakes to the big cities of Chicago and Detroit. The pine logs were used for city homes and other buildings. The loggers took only the choice trees, leaving piles of flammable waste in the forests. Within several decades, the UP's marshes and forests had all burned, sometimes for weeks.

In the 1930s, the Civilian Conservation Corps began replanting the forest, though typically with the fastest-growing trees—the red pines—rather than a mix of what grew here before the settlers came. Then papermaking factories emerged along the Great Lakes shorelines, where trees could readily be found for making the paper, waste from the process could conveniently be dumped into the lakes and rivers, and merchandise could easily be shipped down the lakes and rivers to the cities. Although papermaking companies are working to improve their practices, dioxin, a carcinogenic by-product of papermaking, exists in lakes and in the bodies of fish, fowl, and humans today.

Even factories thousands of miles away affect this land. Some 5,000 pounds of airborne mercury are annually deposited onto the Great Lakes. Mercury, a naturally occurring chemical, is used to manufacture industrial catalysts, solvents, pesticides, light switches, lamps, batteries, paints, preservatives, cosmetics, pharmceuticals, and other products. Trash and medical waste incineration, coal combustion, and other industrial practices release mercury into the environment. Toxic methylmercury, the form most available in the aquatic food chain, can inflict compounded levels of harm on species, especially as it moves to the top of the food chain. Fish-eating birds such as the common loon, osprey, bald eagle, and kingfisher, all residents of the UP, are ingesting higher levels of mercury than they normally would obtain in the natural environment. Research shows this mercury overload can harm the reproductive abilities of these species.

The United States banned the use of PCBs and DDT in the 1970s, but these two chemicals continue to cause problems in the Great Lakes ecosystem. DDT, widely used as a pesticide, caused the thinning of bald eagle and peregrine falcon eggshells, which then broke before chicks could hatch. The federal government placed the peregrine falcon and bald eagle on the Endangered Species List, and scientists are working to restore their populations in the United States. Recent research shows that the cumulative effects of these and other chemicals: They cause cancer and harm the reproductive capacities not only of fish, but also of the humans who eat the fish. DDT and PCBs can persist in fish and other animals for decades.

Alien species—plants and animals that humans have inadvertently or deliberately introduced into areas where they historically never lived—also threaten the UP's balance of flora and fauna. One example is the rainbow smelt. Introduced to Michigan's inland waters as food for stocked salmon in the early 1900s, the rainbow smelt, a small ocean fish, soon escaped to Lake Michigan. By 1930, the rapidly growing smelt population had expanded into Lakes Huron and Superior. The smelt proliferated, choking the native populations of herring and whitefish, whose numbers have drastically declined during the past half century. Today, Whitefish Point and Whitefish Bay are nearly misnomers.

Wild lands and native wildlife still exist in the UP, and they are getting help from many sources. Ninety-six-thousand-acre Seney National Wildlife Refuge in the central part of the UP is a prime example of how some areas have been revitalized. Before settlement, the Seney region abounded with pines, spruces, and open marshes. Logging brought the pines tumbling down, falling one after another into the soggy marshes. When almost all the trees were felled, the loggers sold the land to potential farmers. What was once a logger's dream became a farmer's nightmare. The sandy, wet soil and short growing season made farming nearly impossible. One by one, farmers went bankrupt, and the land was claimed by the state for back taxes. The Michigan government made a decision that would prove to be a great boon to the bird species that had once bred in the forests and marshes near Seney. The state, along with the U.S. government, decided to create a wildlife refuge.

In the 1930s, the Civilian Conservation Corps constructed one hundred miles of dikes that today impound seven thousand acres of water on the refuge. Scientists regulate water flow at these dikes to provide habitat for bald eagles, sandhill cranes, black terns, ospreys, and common loons. Black bears and bobcats live in the surrounding woods. Wet meadow sedges attract Le Conte's sparrows, sedge wrens, and elusive rails that sing when dusk gives way to night. Today, this 95,455-acre refuge protects marsh, swamp, bog, and forest habitat for more than 200 bird species.

About 100 miles east of Seney, researchers and birders, after a long struggle, have preserved dozens of square miles of the Whitefish

Peninsula in the northeastern UP. The area offers a temporary home and abundant food for migrating birds. The Whitefish Point Bird Observatory is providing useful data on the songbirds, waterfowl, and raptors that use the area as a place to stop during migration or to nest. Whitefish Point and Seney are just two examples of places in the UP where The Nature Conservancy, the Michigan Nature Association, government agencies, and many other groups and individuals are working to restore and protect Michigan's Upper Peninsula and the Great Lakes ecosystems.

Because of these conservation efforts, birders can find myriad habitats attracting avian species in the UP. There are dry uplands with pines on which the spruce grouse, a chicken-size bird, may be sitting peacefully nibbling on a pine needle. Sloping woods lead to a glacial lake where a bald eagle flies above a raft of goldeneyes, common mergansers, and ring-necked ducks. In a pine forest, gray jays, common ravens, boreal chickadees, pine siskins, and red-breasted nuthatches tap tree bark for sustenance. There are soggy areas with gnarly brush, where the tiny winter wren hides; he sings his most unusual and varied tinkling song—rapid high pitches that ring clearly in the moist, early spring air. River backwaters support hermit thrushes that pierce the silence with their melancholy ballads, and rushing falls mask the sounds of eastern phoebes singing their names in maple/fir woodlands.

Visitors to the UP can find a mosaic of forest, wetlands, rocky cliffs, dune ridges, and karsts. They can enjoy some of the twelve thousand miles of rivers and streams, two hundred fifty natural waterfalls, four thousand inland lakes, and seventeen hundred miles of sandy and rocky shoreline amid copper mining and logging operations, universities, and resort areas.

A journey through the UP gives but a nanosecond's glimpse into the geological and natural history of a region between Lake Superior above, Lake Michigan below, and Lake Huron to the east. Here, the spruce grouse makes a home among abundant pines providing nourishment in vitamin-rich needles. The common loon catches fish in a large glacial lake stocked with enough food to feed its young. Here, too, the yellow rail builds its hidden nest in a marsh brimming with the sedges the bird needs to raise fledglings. Where cliffs pierce the shoreline along the northwestern edge of the UP, peregrine falcons—reintroduced by humans to one of their native breeding spots—dive for prey. Safe within the deep forest, a male blackburnian warbler chants wheezy songs atop a tree to attract a female to build a nest. The male sharp-tailed grouse finds open space where it joins others in a ritualistic, high-powered courtship dance.

Where water flows brown from the tannic acid deposited by eastern hemlocks, the white-throated sparrows sing *Oh sweet Canada, Canada* and black-throated blue warblers declare *Zray zray zray zray zee* from the gentle slopes along a river. Red-breasted mergansers teach their young to find food in the river. In the last throes of daylight, a tawny, brown thrush, the veery, sings its haunting, downward-spiraling song among the hemlocks that hug the banks of a gently flowing waterfall.

The landscape, like the migrating birds, ebbs and flows with slow yet steady changes. At Grand Sable Dunes near Pictured Rocks National Lakeshore, "ghost forests" show clearly how ephemeral are the dunes. The wind blows the sand, sometimes burying hundreds of pines, and the trees suffocate under the heavy weight of the sand. Hundreds of years later, as the sand shifts, these trees become exposed again, but by this time the trees are barren, dead, mere skeletons of their former selves. And yet, they provide food for black-backed woodpeckers and other birds that rely on dead trees from which to glean insects. Over time, trees will grow here again, regenerating into another forest and creating nesting habitat for other birds, such as the black-throated green warblers. Even the cliffs that rise from the lakes will not last, yielding to erosion over thousands of years, just as the mountains eroded during prehistoric times.

All that lives, dies, and decays within the confines of this ecosystem has a story to tell. Into this rare and wild area, avian researchers have come, hoping to contribute to its ceaseless existence.

Sharp-shinned Hawk

The Birds That Fell from the Sky

A T THE TOP OF A FIFTY-FOOT-TALL DUNE overlooking Whitefish Bay in mid-March, Mary Teesdale wears a brimmed hat and sunglasses beneath the cloudless sky. Her feet sink into boots, good to forty degrees below zero. She stands next to a wooden shack big enough to fit one, maybe two persons.

Like Teesdale's clothing, the weather seems incongruous. The wind blows out of the south in the morning. It rains. At noon, the wind abruptly changes to the northwest and blasts at forty miles per hour. It snows. Whitefish Bay in the northeastern UP remains nearly frozen.

No hawks.

Teesdale listens to the gnashing, snarling ice. Heavy chunks that look like quartz crystals crash together. Like an unhatched bird, the lake struggles to emerge.

The hawks wait to fly.

Thousands of years of instinct signal to the hawks when the wind direction and timing is right to fly to a place where they can find food in winter and space to breed in summer.

While the hawks wait to fly, raptor ecologists like Teesdale wait to count them. The counters endure cold, drizzle, snow, fog, chill-to-the-bone days.

Scanning. No birds. Scanning. No birds. More scanning. No birds.

Then, the winds change. In one afternoon, sixty red-tailed hawks soar overhead while one hundred sharp-shinned hawks dart and turn, riding an invisible, curving roller coaster. A golden eagle floats effortlessly on the wind.

Someone dares wish for more. A peregrine falcon perhaps? Teesdale's reply: "It's on back order. Send money for shipping and handling to the hawk counter."

Each year, Whitefish Point Bird Observatory, founded in 1979, hires biologists to count hawks, eagles, waterbirds, and songbirds in spring and in fall. Affiliated with the Michigan Audubon Society, the observatory began unofficially in the 1950s and 1960s when a group of volunteer birders and bird banders thought their research could be formalized to provide important data that would help sustain populations of the birds they loved.

Whitefish Point is the perfect place to gather data on migrating birds. Tens of thousands of sharp-shinned, Cooper's, rough-legged, and broad-winged hawks; peregrine falcons, kestrels, and merlins; golden and bald eagles; and other raptor species pass here annually during spring migration to their northern breeding grounds, and in fall to their wintering grounds. The Whitefish Peninsula, a tapered promontory, juts into Lake Superior to define the northwestern edge of Whitefish Bay. Its unique shape concentrates birds—including hawks, owls, songbirds, and myriad waterfowl—during fall and spring migration.

The sheer numbers attract birders to witness their passage, but the sheer numbers also mean work for researchers. Through counting and banding, researchers can determine the species composition and the pathways of migrating raptors at Whitefish Point. Their data can also reflect trends in species populations. Banders monitor and assess the health of a raptor population by examining the age and gender of captured and released migrants, or by testing for contaminants, which might offer clues about the effects of pollution on plants and animals.

North America is home to twenty-six species of raptors, including four eagles, five kites, and seventeen different hawks. Sixteen raptor species migrate through the eastern United States. All share characteristics that enable them to prey on mice, lizards, birds, and other animals. A raptor has a short, round head and strong feet with sharply curved talons to strike, snatch, and kill prey. Its hooked and pointed upper bill enables it to tear apart prey for easier consumption.

The ability to kill an animal, sometimes nearly as large as itself, makes a raptor seem formidable, perhaps even invulnerable. Yet habitat destruction, pesticide use, and human misconceptions about these creatures have caused some populations to dwindle. It is a bittersweet experience to count the hawks at Whitefish Point. Dozens of years of data already show a decline in sharp-shinned hawks and other raptor species, even after the banning of DDT.

Seasonal researchers at the observatory are typically young scientists itching to develop their skills, interns earning biology degrees, and biologists migrating to new research projects. Others are veteran volunteers who help run the observatory as young scientists move on to new territories.

For at least fifteen years, Mary Teesdale maintained her home base near Charlevoix, Michigan, one hundred miles southeast of Whitefish Bay. Teesdale traveled to Whitefish Point every March to count the hawks until June. But like the hawks she has counted, Teesdale is always on the move, one winter monitoring grassland birds' habitats, another migration season counting hawks (seven hundred eighty thousand of them in twelve days in Veracruz, Mexico—"We went home happy," she says) and now doing breeding bird surveys at Lewis and Clark National Forest in Montana, where she has access to a phone or a computer only on Friday nights and where she pitches her own tent four to five days a week in the middle of the woods amid rainstorms, snowstorms, and winds that can destroy her only living quarters.

Teesdale says she's always been the adventurous, independent sort—climbing trees while growing up in northern Michigan, racing in downhill ski tournaments, managing her own stained-glass art business in Charlevoix and then deciding one spring, after visiting Whitefish Point Bird Observatory, that she was going to be a hawk counter. "I just really wanted to do that," says Teesdale at her weekend bunkhouse in the Montana forest. So she spent three seasons sitting on the dunes with counters, learning and reading books until she gained the knowledge to apply for and get the job, as well as several other jobs there, including banding owls in spring and songbirds in fall. "I discovered how fascinating it was the whole season to watch migration go by and the plants start to emerge, one by one, and then summer into fall migration," says the short, blonde-haired woman, who defines success not with dollars but with the joy of doing what she loves. Adding Whitefish Point Bird Observatory biologist to her resume gave Teesdale the ability to secure more research assignments. These jobs, combined with some life savings and parental support, allow her to survive financially.

Teesdale came to the observatory knowing what she would endure—standing next to a wooden shack, going inside every so often to keep warm, recording data while answering questions from curious visitors and birders who walk a long boardwalk and up forty-one wooden steps to the sand dune that offers a good view of the hawks flying over the Point. Down below, at the Point's edge along the lakeshore, waterfowl counters enjoy a slightly more hospitable environment. But they still must endure the brittle wind of the Point as they count the thousands of migrating loons and ducks flying low along the water, away from the hawks and eagles that might enjoy a duck for lunch. Temperatures hovered below normal when Adam Byrne came to count ducks and geese in 1997. He stood there in what he called "seemingly endless north winds."

When the winds changed, the waterfowl came in record numbers. In 1997, from April 15 to May 31, waterbird biologists tallied 42,260 birds of sixty-four species during 366 hours of observation—common loons, white-winged scoters, red-breasted mergansers, Canada geese, oldsquaws, greater scaups, and other ducks.

Meanwhile, the raptor ecologists counted hawks from atop the dune.

Relying on the Lake Superior and Whitefish Bay shoreline as a landmark, waterfowl and raptors steadily fly north to their breeding grounds. For hawks, these bodies of water represent the last barrier before they reach Canada. Hawks typically avoid flying over large bodies of water when migrating. Land and water features create a natural narrow corridor, funneling the birds directly to Whitefish Point as they travel through the Great Lakes region. When they reach the Point, seventeen miles from Canada, the hawks decide either to fly over the lake or to attempt a different route. Some of the raptors continue flying, perhaps perishing; others remain for an hour, a day, or longer, feasting on migratory songbirds also trapped in the funnel. This makes for an exciting birding experience as sharp-shinned hawks dip and dive into the jack pines lining the shoreline, snatching white-throated sparrows and other songbirds. Birders may count thousands of raptors flying near the Point in a single day during migration.

Each raptor fills a migratory niche, entering the Point at various times depending on where and when it winters, what it eats, and its size, flying skills, sex, and age. These factors contribute to what seems to be a choreography in which the largest raptors, for the most part, come first. One theory suggests the smaller raptors follow the larger ones to avoid becoming their prey. Regardless of the reason, it's the masters of the sky, the bald and golden eagles, that come first in mid-March, one or two at a time, followed by goshawks, also single or in small groups, and then red-tailed hawks and rough-legged hawks with their broad wings and large bodies. Then come the smaller sharp-shinned hawks, dozens at a time. The sharpie numbers peak in late April. Then the fast fliers, the peregrine falcons, come, and finally, large kettles, or congregations, of broad-winged hawks in late May.

Sharp-shinned, Cooper's, red-tailed, red-shouldered, and broad-winged hawks fly across the dunes toward Whitefish Bay and then retreat to land to ponder the situation. Bald eagles, northern harriers, rough-legged hawks, northern goshawks, and merlins flap more than they soar, and some may be able to make the trip across the bay. A peregrine falcon comes out of nowhere, flying swiftly and effortlessly across the dune and over the bay. Recognizing these differences in flight styles helps hawk counters identify species. By the end of her first season, Mary Teesdale had experienced the joy of announcing that a tiny dot in the sky is a bald eagle. She had also developed an affinity for raptors that could only be shared with fellow hawk counters. After all, they know what it is like to endure lonely days on the dune when no hawk flies by and no human appears, frustrating times when too many humans arrive and disturb the scientific process, and exhilarating moments when it seems no one can come between a counter and a wild bird.

Possessing a migratory spirit seems to be a common characteristic of raptor ecologists. They go with the wind, never getting too tied to one place, and yet immersing themselves in their work, focused solely on the research. They share a kinship with their subjects, who rarely stay in the same place for more than several months.

In mid-March, Teesdale begins her daily routine counting hawks at the dune, recording information not only on a data sheet, but also more informally in a diary:

March 18: I do a lot of calisthenics and jumping around to stay warm. I have to be aware every second, waiting for the bird. Gyrfalcon, I have in mind. Battling the cold, I wait for the gyrfalcon.

Like the other counters on the dune and the banders stationed in a blind nearby, Teesdale conscientiously records information and wonders what she might contribute to the wide realm of research on the world's birds of prey. Nearly a century ago, Norman Wood, a research biologist with the George Shiras expedition, counted hawks here, too. He had no heated shack to enter periodically for warmth, no birders to keep him company. In 1914 from May 13 to June 13, Wood counted hundreds of sharp-shinned hawks migrating northward. As Wood reveled in the wonder of these magnificent raptors, he also found many dead hawks that bounty collectors and hunters shot during migration flights. Wood found hundreds of dead red-tailed hawks in May of 1914. The U.S. government paid a hefty bounty to those who shot thousands of red-tailed, broad-winged, sharp-shinned, and Cooper's hawks.

The birds fell from the sky like shooting stars, then lay lifeless on the dunes.

Humans erroneously thought raptors hunted sheep, pigs, goats, and other farm animals, thus damaging a farmer's livelihood. In 1927, a Detroit newspaper published a photograph of a man standing beside a waist-high pile of hawks, which he had shot in one day for a bounty of fifty cents per head.

Bird researchers began to wonder about the slaughter of hawks at Whitefish Point and other places in North America. Would there be any birds left for them to study? In 1934, protesting scientists at a raptor migration spot in Pennsylvania called Hawk Mountain urged the U.S. government to repeal the bounty it was paying for dead hawks. By then people were beginning to understand that hawks were not the loathsome sheep and poultry killers they had thought them to be. Little did they know that in a few short decades, these raptors would also teach humans about what is happening to our environment and perhaps to us. Indeed, it was the eagle and the falcon that alerted humans to the harmful effects of the pesticide DDT.

In the 1960s, scientists noticed that bald eagle and peregrine falcon populations were declining. They found the birds were not reproducing because eggshells were too thin to support the life inside, so the young never hatched. Scientists linked the eggshell-thinning to DDT contamination. Eagles, falcons, and other raptors are at the top of the food chain. When the foods they eat—fish, birds, and land animals—become contaminated with DDT sprayed on crops and water, the DDT accumulates in the fatty tissue of eagles, peregrines, and other species at the top of the food chain. The females pass these contaminants on through their eggs. The United States banned the use of DDT in 1972 and placed the bald eagle and peregrine falcon on the federal Endangered Species List, while scientists devised ways to bring these species back from the edge of extinction.

Would humans have discovered the problems with DDT had it not been for the eagles and falcons? No one can be certain, but had the bounty not been repealed, had humans not started counting hawks instead of shooting them, the DDT story could be very different today.

Bald eagle populations have rebounded, but the U.S. Fish and Wildlife Service reclassified the species from endangered to threatened in 1995, meaning its breeding status has improved but not fully recovered. The U.S. Fish and Wildlife Service proposed removing the falcon from the Federal Endangered Species List in 1999. Scientists are still studying the potential cumulative effects of DDT on human reproduction, as well as the effects various other pesticides still in use today may have on raptors. We need researchers like Teesdale and others to maintain a watchful vigil at places like Whitefish Point Bird Observatory.

To monitor raptor populations, the U.S. Fish and Wildlife Service initiated a hawk census project in 1979. The project enabled Whitefish Point Bird Observatory to hire its first full-time hawk counter, Alan Ryff. He tallied 20,744 hawks, eagles, and vultures between April 24 and May 27 that year. Subsequent counts show that between 5,000 and 14,000 sharp-shinned hawks pass over Whitefish Point each spring. An average of 75 turkey vultures, 139 ospreys, 45 bald eagles, 307 northern harriers, 65 Cooper's hawks, 124 northern goshawks, 31 red-shouldered hawks, 3,844 broad-winged hawks, 1,370 red-tailed hawks, 859 rough-legged hawks, 19 golden eagles, 426 American kestrels, 43 merlins, and 18 peregrine falcons have been counted from March 15 to May 31 between 1983 and 1989.

March 25: An icy, foggy morning. A quarter-inch of rime covers everything. The sun appears. Everything sparkles and drips. A single ship, the Herbert C. Jackson, *comes by.*

One mid-March day, while serenaded by the raspy caw of ravens, Teesdale walked up to the shack on the dune where she would count hawks. Struggling to open the shack's iced-over door, Teesdale immediately understood why the advertisement for the hawk-counting job stated that "those who dislike cold and windy conditions need not apply." The wind burned her face as she forced open the door. Inside, a six-inch layer of ice had built up on the floor during the long, cold winter, as snow blew into any crack it could find.

But you can find paradise in cold places.

A pinpoint in the sky. "A bald eagle," Teesdale sings.

The bald eagle is flying now to a place up north where it can breed; its breeding range extends from Alaska, Canada, and the Great Lakes, south to Florida and California. It will not breed until it has reached four or five years of age and has acquired full adult plumage: snow white head, dark body, and white tail. When spring comes, the bald eagle flies north to lakes and mighty rivers where abundant fish will feed its young. Together the male and female bald eagle build a huge nest of sticks, laden with mosses, pine needles, feathers, and grasses to house two eggs that hatch in about thirty-five days. Eaglets are dependent on their parents much longer than young songbirds are and cannot even fly until seventy-two or more days after they hatch. Once they have learned to hunt on their own, they will migrate south where there is open water in winter. Though the bald eagle may look majestic and strong it endures many hardships during its life, including finding its own winter territory to fish and warding off other hungry eagles.

The golden eagle faces its own challenges. A half-century ago, people thought golden eagles mainly ate livestock, so between 1940 and 1962, sheep raisers killed twenty thousand golden eagles. In 1962, federal law made it illegal to shoot golden eagles. Then a study in 1971 showed that golden eagles mainly eat rabbits, snakes, turtles, great horned owls, and other animals living in the grasslands where it breeds.

The male and female golden eagle build either an elaborate nest of sticks, lichens, and branches or a mere circle of branches on a cliff shelf overlooking grassy areas. The pair often use the same nest site each year, adding sticks to maintain its sturdiness. The female lays two eggs, which hatch in forty-five days. The golden eaglets remain in the nest for another two months, and depend on their parents for food another month after that. The inexperienced juveniles may perish even before their first migration. Many still are shot or trapped illegally.

It is a rare day indeed when a Whitefish Point raptor biologist spots a golden eagle. She knows it's an eagle because of its steady, effortless flight, its way of appearing in the sky unannounced as if it came from the parting heavens. Separating the bald from the golden eagles requires experience. "Bald eagles spread their wings flat to glide and soar," Mary Teesdale says. "Golden eagles hold their wings in a slight upturn or dihedral." Some visitors nod their heads; others are still baffled by Teesdale's apparent special power to declare "Bald eagle!" with such confidence as a pinpoint of a raptor glides above their amazed eyes.

But there is no time to dally and converse with visitors. Raptor season has begun. The counters must count.

April 1: For the first four hours, it is nonstop harriers, rough-legs, and sharp-shins. And 122 red-tails. Over 200 hawks for the day. Every kind but broad-wings and peregrines. It seems like a river of birds streaming by. On my back, I look at the white bellies of high-flying red-tails shining like stars in the daytime. I am not restless. I sit in my spot, and watch the birds and time move by me. I see everything, their perfect feathers moving with almost imperceptible adjustments to catch or spill the winds. The red-tails can click open their wings or tails like a fan. They're hungry and hunting and screaming.

The red-tailed hawk, North America's most common buteo, sports broad wings that can spread to twenty-five inches and possesses excellent soaring skills. Only the adult has the characteristic red tail. A juvenile has a thinly banded tail with a single, wider, darker band near the end and large, white, translucent squares on the outer part of its wings. Many of the red-tails seen at Whitefish Point display dark banding on their bellies, a fairly good identification mark and something Teesdale can see when she is on her back staring at the sky.

Of the four species of buteos—red-tailed, broad-winged, red-shouldered, and rough-legged hawks—that cross Whitefish Point, red-tails probably elicit the least excitement. "Another red-tail," someone says in a ho-hum way. When hawks are scarce, counters spend time observing red-tailed hawk flight and determining the subspecies, something that cannot easily be done for the other raptors at Whitefish Point. For instance, the rare Harlan's red-tailed hawk, once considered a separate species, is the darkest of several red-tail subspecies and breeds in southern Canada. Whether a Harlan's red-tailed hawk has ever been accurately recorded here is a source of discussion on the dune. "I'm not convinced we have a valid record," says Jim Granlund, one of the founders of Whitefish Point Bird Observatory. "Probably the Harlan's we have seen in the past were rufous or dark-phase western red-tails," he says. Teesdale says she and several other hawk counters saw a Harlan's red-tail at the Point; they are convinced that's what it was. So even a red-tail can lead to interesting discourse—and the melancholy scream of this cosmopolitan species coupled with its mating ritual can strike an emotional chord in even the most seasoned birder.

Kreeeee-er, calls the male red-tailed hawk on its nesting grounds in open country throughout the United States. The male, smaller than the female, soars high, screams, then suddenly dives swiftly at the female. She then turns over in the air and opens her claws to intertwine with the male's in a fascinating courtship display. By late April in the UP, the male and female red-tailed hawks may be building a bulky nest of twigs and sticks in an oak or pine tree. After about a month of incubation, the young hatch. When they are about forty-five days old, the fledglings are ready to leave the nest and partake in a banquet of grasshoppers, mice, squirrels, rabbits, moles, chipmunks, snakes, lizards, and salamanders. This eclectic diet could explain why the red-tailed hawk has better adapted to various habitats than its other raptor cousins. But food can become scarce even for this generalist, and when it's hard to find, the red-tailed hawk migrates elsewhere, sometimes in flocks, to search for sustenance. No raptor is immune to nature's abrupt changes or human activities.

April 27: Sharpies are flying all over first thing in the morning. Two hundred sixty-six sharpies the first hour. They just kept pouring in from the west and filtering around the shore and heading south. A river of hawks. We ended up with 1,074. The sky to the west looked like a bee swarm all day until the last hour. This is a dangerous place for small birds.

While Teesdale is clicking off sharpies, Brenda and Richard Keith are banding these and other hawks that fall into the special mist nets behind the Whitefish Point bird-banding station. The Keiths begin in late April and work for five weeks, a period that corresponds with the sharp-shin migration. Banding begins at sunrise and lasts until nearly sundown. "On days when large numbers of sharpies come in, it's like a feeding frenzy—they fall out of the sky," says Brenda. "Cloudy, foggy days bring the birds down. On a clear day, birds stay higher. Once they have expended the energy to reach that height, they won't come down to us. Also, if it's too windy or the wind is coming from the wrong direction, the birds aren't flying."

The sharp-shinned hawk, like all accipiters, has shorter wings and a longer tail than the buteos, and thus greater maneuverability in the woods. An accipiter flies with steady wing beats interrupted by occasional glides. Comparing a buteo to an accipiter helps explain how many different species of raptors can survive in the same world. Each has its niche, feeding in particular ways, in particular habitats, and upon particular species. While buteos circle high in the air watching the ground for mice and other prey upon which to swoop, accipiters—including the sharp-shinned hawk, Cooper's hawk, and goshawk—feed mainly on smaller birds, darting through woodlands and grasping a surprised wood thrush in their fierce talons.

Both the sharp-shinned and Cooper's hawks have a long, slender body with long, slender bright yellow legs, white underparts barred with reddish brown, a bluish gray back, and finely streaked throat. The sharpie often shows a square to slightly forked tail, while the Cooper's tail appears rounder. That difference alone, however, does not distinguish the two, especially in the sky. Birders watch for other clues such as the longer extension of the head in front of the wings on the Cooper's hawk compared with the sharp-shinned.

The female sharp-shin builds a nest of sticks and twigs lined with bark strips in a branch next to a tree trunk, usually in a conifer. She lays four to five eggs, which both she and her mate incubate. The young hatch in thirty-four to thirty-five days and fledge twenty-three days after that. The Cooper's hawk, which will not tolerate a sharp-shinned hawk in its territory, nests in pine and hardwood groves and farther south than the sharp-shinned does, so their habitats don't entirely overlap. Sharp-shinned and Cooper's hawks have also suffered from pesticide contamination. In 1971, scientists reported drastic declines in their populations. They apparently were suffering the same fate as the bald eagle and peregrine falcon, and some states placed sharp-shinned and Cooper's hawks on their endangered or threatened species list. The states make these decisions based on data like that gathered by the Keiths.

The Keiths band hawks in a makeshift station, a wooden structure with a four-inch-wide viewing area camouflaged by pines. Unless you know where the hawk nets are, you can rarely find the Keiths during banding season. If it's going to be a good day for banding, they arrive early in the morning and remain until late afternoon. A sign posted at the trailhead to the banding station warns that people should shout their presence and not come any closer until Richard yells "OK" from the pines.

The Keiths, both dark-haired and of medium build and height, talk freely about their intense love of birds and banding, and the controversies that surround this once mainly recreational endeavor. Ever since John James Audubon fit a bird with a band in the late 1800s to see if it would return the next year, bird banders have debated why they do what they do. Some people band purely for sport with no intention of collecting useful data, say the Keiths. They band for the chance to hold a wild bird in their hand. But bird banding is becoming more scientific and goal oriented now. To receive a bird-banding permit today, a person has to show how the data they collect will be used.

"You have to consider the bird first. It can't be a macho thing," says Brenda, who thinks birds can actually sense a bander's motive, whether it is for sport or part of the process of saving a species or an individual. "Some bird banders love birds, but I'm not sure they have any other goals," she says. "We love birds and we are doing banding in a useful manner. It's a different era of banding now. Now you have to have a reason to band—scientific study. We feel that's our mission. And to educate."

"Nobody knows for sure if what we're doing can answer questions and help birds," says Richard. "But the only way to find answers is through concrete, consistent, standardized data-gathering techniques."

Coming to that realization, however, takes years of getting to know birds and ecosystems. Neither Brenda nor Richard is formally trained in biology, but each has years of experience as volunteers and paid workers, and they have proven their worth in the bird-banding community. Brenda, who grew up in a rural Michigan town, says her parents, especially her mother, sparked her interest in birds. Brenda started identifying the birds that came to the family feeders, and then she began looking at bird books and realized she could find even more kinds of avian creatures besides those that came to the feeders.

She recalls her first foray into the UP: "When I was four years old, my family took a trip to the UP. We were visiting all the tourist places, like Tahquamenon Falls. And that's where I got my first pair of binoculars and saw my first bald eagle." That was the day, she says, she became a birder.

Brenda did not return to the UP until 1981, after she met Richard, who had more recently discovered the joys of birding and bird banding. In the late 1970s, after a serious motorcycle accident, Richard took long walks as part of his rehabilitation. One day in the woods he saw a large, red-crested bird with stark, black-and-white wings. A bird book revealed it was a pileated woodpecker, an attractive, deep-woods bird that can easily make a birder of a human.

Richard began scouting birds, learning their names, and meeting people who enjoyed the hobby. His new interest soon propelled him into a life dedicated to studying and helping these winged animals. Richard says he was inspired by his mentor, Ray Adams, the research director for the Kalamazoo Nature Center, near where the Keiths live.

"Ray Adams has a master banding permit," says Richard. "He has been banding for twenty-five years. He's completely dedicated."

"Anyone who wants to be a bird bander needs to work with someone like Ray Adams," says Brenda. "You have to be careful," she says. "You have to work with someone who knows what they are doing."

Now Richard spends twelve hundred hours each year banding birds for the Kalamazoo Nature Center. As the center's bird-banding coordinator, Richard oversees five paid banders and twenty-five volunteers who band songbirds from September through November every day of the week in southern Michigan. In summer, Richard bands birds in Michigan for the Monitoring Avian Productivity and Survivorship program, known as MAPS, which is run by the California-based Institute for Bird Populations. Richard works three days per week banding birds that drop into twenty-four carefully placed nets.

As a board member for the Whitefish Point Bird Observatory, Richard says he is thrilled that the observatory is working with the Canadian Migration Monitoring Network to analyze bird migration and banding data from many northern sites, a project that is crucial to raptor and songbird survival.

Like many researchers, the Keiths get paid for some of the work they do; the rest of the time, they volunteer. For example, Brenda gets paid for three months by the Kalamazoo Nature Center to band birds in the fall, and runs one of the MAPS banding stations in the summer as a volunteer. "Brenda is every bit as dedicated as I am," says Richard, "especially with the paperwork," which he says is the most important part of banding. Only on paper can a researcher begin to see trends such as population declines.

To supplement their income, Richard and Brenda operate a small business that manufactures shepherd's crook poles for hanging bird feeders. Come sharp-shin season, they leave the business to spend their spring banding birds at Whitefish Point or to instruct younger banders who may one day assume their work.

Inside a small wooden blind, the Keiths have arranged Pringles potato chip cans they use to temporarily contain the larger female sharp-shins, and Coca-Cola cans to hold the smaller males, as well as a few coffee cans just in case they catch larger birds of prey, though the nets are designed to trap the sharpies. When they retrieve a hawk from the net, the Keiths place the bird in a proper size can, where it is dark and the birds feel relatively safe. The banders can then safely and efficiently complete their work.

"There's a shin right overhead," says Brenda, quietly. "He's circling."

Moments later, the "shin" drops into the net. Richard quickly removes the net from the bird's tail while grasping its powerful feet. He frees the bird's head next. Then he frees the wings and puts a bander's hold on the bird enclosing the tail, legs, and wing tips to immobilize it. Richard calls it the Popsicle hold. It helps keep the sharp talons from piercing his skin. Of the 520 hawks the Keiths banded one year, 480 were sharp-shins that had to be measured, weighed, aged, and sexed. That's a lot of sharpie talons to avoid.

Richard gently examines the sharp-shin he just retrieved from the net. "This is definitely an adult," he says. Red eyes, indicating adulthood, glare at him. "It's probably an after-second-year bird. If it was a third-year, we would find one or more rufous-edged feathers on its rump or back."

"This bird hasn't eaten," says Richard, examining its crop, the bulge in the throat where food is stored while being digested. Sharp-shin crops can sometimes be the size of golf balls.

"They are such hunters," says Brenda, measuring the length of the outstretched wing, or wing chord. "Hunger is not the driving force. Instinct is."

Sharp-shin migration follows a distinct pattern. Female sharp-shins arrive on the heels of their prey, the white-throated sparrows. But the male sharp-shins wait until most of the females have migrated. Is that because the smaller males might become the females' dinner? No one knows for certain.

The Keiths have recently begun marking each sharpie with a felt-tip pen in the wrist area under the wing. Each day, they use a different color. When they see a sharp-shin overhead, they can easily see and record the color and monitor how long sharp-shins remain at Whitefish Point before continuing their migration.

The Keiths work with researchers from Canada who test blood samples to determine the presence of lead and other chemicals in sharp-shins. "The Canadian researchers are finding that birds are picking up toxins from pesticides used in Central America where they winter," says Richard. "The toxins may be banned here, but we are still making the chemicals and shipping them out of the country. Many people in this line of work feel things are not improving. Some bird populations are on the decline, including the sharp-shins."

The Keiths continue their banding, day after day, recording numbers in columns. Sometimes they are so busy they cannot keep ahead of all the sharpies falling into their nets. Other days, when the raptors are scarce, they focus on the cold sting in their feet and the other birds flying by.

"One day last week, all of a sudden, robins were everywhere, one hundred at a time," says Brenda.

"The blue jays will be here soon," adds Richard. "There will be days when there are over one thousand blue jays flying through here."

They sometimes hear flocks of sandhill cranes rattling overhead. "Once we heard the cranes and as they got closer, we heard Canada geese. And then we heard the cranes again," says Brenda. "We looked up and there was a mixed flock of cranes and geese."

When May comes and the sharp-shin population begins to diminish, the Keiths begin thinking about banding birds back in Kalamazoo, but before they go, they look to the sky for the return of the broad-winged hawk. At the top of the dune, the hawk counters are looking too.

April 29: The broad-wings kettle nicely in several places and stream over several times. Two hundred twenty-four broad-wings.

The flight for which many have been waiting begins.

Broad-winged hawks master the thermals better than any other raptor species. Hot air rising over sun-warmed patches of land attracts the broad-wings, which congregate in kettles of sometimes thousands of birds. Groups of birds migrating together, called kettles, rise as high as they can with one thermal, then glide from the top of the air column to the base of another. At first, counters see one or two kettles of broad-wings. Then, in a day or two, counters and birders see dozens of kettles, with thousands of birds filling the sky from horizon to horizon.

It seems contradictory that broad-wings prefer a company of thousands during migration yet are secretive and solitary during breeding season. Broad-wings nest in the UP and Canada, as well as farther south in states such as Illinois and Wisconsin. On a walk through the UP's murky bogs, a hiker might hear the shrieking, two-syllable courtship cry of the broad-winged hawk.

A sharp, haunting *Pe-Teeee* resounds in the woods. The second syllable is longer, more insistent than the first. Much smaller than the red-tail, the broad-wing stands about as tall as a crow, displaying a barred, reddish brown belly and broad, black-and-white tail band.

The male and female build a lichen-lined nest of twigs, typically near water in woods, often in oaks or pine trees. The female lays two to three eggs. She and her mate incubate the eggs for twenty-one to twenty-five days, then feed the immature birds until they can fly at about forty-one days old. Then the young join their parents and other broad-wings to migrate south for the winter.

While raptor ecologists expect to count thousands of broad-winged hawks in a single season at the Point, they are lucky if they count fifty goshawks.

The adult northern goshawk, an accipiter with a conspicuous dark eyebrow behind a red eye, a dark crown, bluish gray back, and a wingspan of up to forty-seven inches, flies through tangled forests using its long tail and rounded wings to turn sharply. Its powerful talons quickly kills hares, squirrels, ducks, and other prey. The goshawk follows the ten-year population cycle of the snowshoe hare, its main prey. When the snowshoe hare population declines, the goshawk population declines accordingly. Then the species irrupts, or invades an area other than its typical breeding and wintering range, flying as far south as Illinois. Data from Whitefish Point show that goshawks irrupted in the winter of 1982–83 and that numbers were fairly low for nine years after that. So it followed that a goshawk invasion was due there the winter of 1992–93.

It never happened.

One reason could be that an abundance of ruffed grouse provided a secondary food source to the goshawks and dampened the peak of irruption. Or it could be that bad weather kept the goshawks from coming into the UP and that instead they irrupted in Duluth, Minnesota, where an unusually high number of goshawks were seen that season. Regardless, the absence of higher-than-normal numbers of goshawks that season suggests that the most carefully researched scientific data cannot always foreshadow what nature will do.

When the number of raptors flying over the Point begins to ebb, the researchers experience a sad sense of finality, a foreshadowing of the end of hawk migration. On June 1, Mary Teesdale's second-to-last day of counting, she logs fifty-nine broad-wings, a few sharpies, a bald eagle, and two red-tails. She has time to wonder about those who stop at the dune for just a few hours, while she is there eight or more hours per day.

She senses an uneasiness in the visitors. Perhaps that is because "coming here brings close to home the largest flaw in their lifestyle—the absence of wildness or freedom," she says.

Teesdale has chosen her own lifestyle of freedom to roam with the birds. That comes with a price—occasional loneliness. That loneliness is never more acute than at the end of hawk-counting season or the end of another research project.

June 1: I have been washed by the winds of Superior for three months. I have danced with them, laughed, breathed, and almost blown away with them. These winds have different voices and temperatures. To resist them is to freeze. That is the secret of keeping warm. Embrace the wind. Embrace the day. Or hide in the trees.

Northern Saw-whet Owl

Midnight Banders

THE SUN SINKS INTO LAKE SUPERIOR at Whitefish Point, leaving behind an orange glow mingling with a cerulean blue sky on a clear, cold, windless night. At the top of the hawk dune where we counted raptors by day, we watch for the silhouette of an owl to pulse across the changing horizon. A shivering quiet perforates the air as dusk fades quickly to darkness and clear vision becomes nearly impossible.

Two gulls scold their way across the shore until they are out of sight. Silence again.

Then, a long, slender, dark form flaps like a huge moth across the dune and disappears over the lake.

It came from behind; it might have been roosting in the pines just south of the Point during the day. But now, this long-eared owl has begun its evening journey north to its Canadian breeding grounds. Perhaps it came from wintering in Texas, then flew to the UP, and is now making its last trek miles across Lake Superior to nest in a pine tree in northern Ontario.

In late April, I'm bundled in layers against the cold, and I wonder what it would be like to fly free at dark with nothing below but a massive body of water, knowing instinctively that steady flight must continue until land is reached. The thought gives me an eerie, unsettled feeling, like being trapped between the warmth of a summer day and the ominous cold of a winter blizzard.

Undulating northern lights fade in and out of the darkness, temporarily changing the course of my thoughts. Then another slender mothlike form flies before the shimmering green sheets of the aurora borealis. The surrealistic moment lasts for seconds. No more owls fly that night. We can no longer see. We retreat to our lighted habitats.

But owl banders at Whitefish Point Bird Observatory, like the owls, are just starting their day. Banders remain awake all night, making hourly runs along fine-meshed mist nets suspended between two poles. They sit, two or three of them, in a ten-foot-by-ten-foot area equipped with essentials: coffee, snacks, neck warmers, aluminum cans of varying sizes in which to place netted owls, and sturdy canvas gloves. The pair of gloves is an optimistic prop, for it will only be used if the formidable great horned owl becomes enmeshed in a net. The banders work from one-half hour after sunset to one-half hour before sunrise, which can add up to twelve long hours in the last throes of winter before the days begin to lengthen.

During these hours, the owls retreat from their daytime roosts to hunt. Hawks and eagles hunt by day, owls hunt by night. In this way, these raptors can share the same feeding habitat.

An owl can see well during the day. But its large, forward-facing eyes surrounded by facial disks also enable it to see remarkably well at night. These features allow a great deal of light to enter the owl's eyes; a third eyelid protects the retina from bright light. Because its eyes are fixed in the skull, an owl must rotate its large head, sometimes up to 270 degrees, to view its surroundings.

An owl's ears play an important part in helping it catch a meal at night. In several owl species, the ears are asymmetrical—one is located higher than the other, helping the owl locate its prey by sound. To understand this phenomenon, find two willing people to help you in an experiment. One of you stands on a chair, another stands on a slightly taller chair. A third stands at the back of the room. The two people on the chair close their eyes. The person at the back of the room squeaks like a mouse. With eyes closed, both people standing on the chair point to where the sound is. Open your eyes and you'll see that between your two points, you've zeroed in on your prey.

Special eyesight is not the only thing an owl has to help it quietly snatch prey in the dark. A serrated fringe on the leading edge of the wing feathers softens the flow of air over the wings and enables an owl to fly almost silently as it swoops to surprise its prey. Its large wings help it fly with slow wing beats; that also helps maintain silent flight.

The owl grabs its prey on the ground or in the air using its sharp, recurved talons. Then it consumes the prey whole or in large portions, regurgitating undigested material such as fur and bones in a pellet. When studied by humans, the pellet reveals what the owl ate. Some other bird species, including some hawks and even robins, also eject pellets.

April through mid-May is the peak owl-watching time at Whitefish Point. Hundreds of owls migrate through the area at night on their way to their northern breeding grounds, while others come from their year-round habitats in the UP to search for food. Of the nineteen species of owls in North America, ten either breed or spend winters in Michigan. Banders have netted northern saw-whet, boreal, great gray, great horned, barred, long-eared, short-eared, and northern hawk-owls at Whitefish Point. Each of these owl species breeds and feeds in varied habitats.

Like the northern goshawk, the boreal, snowy, great gray, and northern hawk-owls have evolved to live in the world's northernmost regions, preying mainly on species confined to those areas. When prey is scarce in winter, these owls fly south to find food, some of them spending the cold season in the UP. When spring comes, the owls fly north, where specific habitats and foods are available for their young. Although the boreal, snowy, great gray, and northern hawk-owl winter in the UP, as of this writing, the only confirmed breeding record in the UP for any of these species is a single successful breeding for the northern hawk-owl in 1905. Birders suspect the great gray may breed in the UP, but no one has proven it.

A few records from the 1980s and 1990s exist for the successful breeding of the short-eared owl in the eastern UP. Five owls—the eastern screech-owl, the great horned, barred, long-eared, and northern saw-whet—regularly breed in the UP. Eastern screech-owls, barred owls, and great horned owls also live and breed in many other parts of the United States, wherever they find suitable habitat. The saw-whet and long-eared owls fly south in winter to find prey, then return to the UP in early spring to breed. In winter, they roost during the day in conifers, perhaps a stand of arborvitae trees in northern Illinois and hunt mainly at night. They return to the UP in early spring to breed, the saw-whets whistling and the long-ears barking to attract mates.

Piecing together the unique patterns of owl movement is complicated, challenging, and exciting. It's a relatively new science—owls are not as easy as hawks to track. Most scientists believe that owl species' numbers are declining. This is especially true for owls with small distribution ranges such as the great gray owl and the northern hawk-owl, according to the Society for the Conservation and Research of Owls, a group based in England with members worldwide. The Ontario Birds at Risk Program, an international initiative, has placed the northern hawk-owl, great gray owl, and short-eared owl on its list of species of special concern. By tracking and banding owls at Whitefish Point Bird Observatory, and at its northern neighbor, Long Point Bird Observatory in Ontario, Canada, researchers are learning more about the fascinating lives of owls and their population trends and cycles.

At the end of April beneath clear skies, owl banders Jacob LaCroix and Susan Marden begin the night's first foray at 9 P.M., one-half hour after unfurling eleven mist nets at the Point. Wind and rain the past few nights kept the banders away from their work. If winds are stronger than twelve miles per hour, or if there is any moisture on the nets, they will not capture and band owls. An owl lacks the oil glands other birds such as waterfowl use to repel moisture from the body. Being caught in a net on a soggy or windy night is not good for an owl's health, so the banders work only during optimum conditions.

The banders wear headlamps, like spelunkers, as they leave for their first net run. The darkness momentarily blinds them. But they know the route. They walk swiftly, purposefully, recognizing familiar branches to follow or a stand of pines to avoid. They turn in harmony, one left, one right, then meet back at the end of one net and proceed to the next. The waves hitting Lake Superior's pebble beach sound like distant drums.

As their eyes get accustomed to darkness, the banders are tempted to look to the clear, crisp sky to find Orion's belt and Cassiopeia, but they focus only on one thing, shining flashlights into each net and hoping an owl is encumbered within. While an owl is on the hunt or preparing to migrate, it may fly into a net and get entangled. Then the banders prod it free, weigh and band it, and send it back into the night.

They find no netted owls during the 9 P.M. walk. "Lately, it has been between 2 and 4 A.M. that we get owls," says LaCroix, a quiet, pensive young man who focuses clearly on his goal, to be the best researcher he can be. Like many young researchers hired to band owls at Whitefish Point Bird Observatory, LaCroix began his career here contentedly living in a small room in a former general store and post office that now houses the observatory's staff and seasonal researchers. Dogsled teams used to leave from the building to head across Whitefish Bay to deliver mail in winter. Today, the observatory's executive director, Russell Utych, maintains a cramped office here where hawk counters, waterbird counters, owl banders, and other observatory researchers share cooking and phone-answering duties and watch reruns of *Star Trek* after being out in the field all day.

The owl banders are the most mysterious of all the researchers at the Point. They work at night and are less self-revealing. They seem as enigmatic as their subjects.

These researchers don't say it, but you can hear it in their voices and see it in their eyes: they believe they are the lucky ones, able to experience nature in a more primitive way than most. At times, they even exude a kind of teenage belief in their own immortality. But they are skillful at gathering data, and they are acutely aware of the many owl researchers who came before them.

Two of these pioneering owl researchers include Alice Kelley and her husband, Neil, who came from the Cranbrook Institute of Science in Bloomfield Hills, Michigan, and the Ontario Bird Banding Association to band hawks at the Point in the 1960s. They gathered data on eye color, age, and other characteristics of sharp-shinned hawks, information that could only be found by banding and measuring birds. These valuable data added to the scientist's limited knowledge of hawks and shed light on a group of species about which scientists knew little—owls.

At dawn on May 6, 1966, while the Kelleys and other researchers were catching owls at a mist-net banding station near the Point, two of the researchers flushed not a hawk but a boreal owl into one of the nets. This rare nocturnal species spends its days roosting on a branch high in a pine tree, where its mottled colors camouflage it from human and nonhuman observers. Seeing the species so close and so unexpectedly engendered an idea. Why not set up the mist nets at night to band owls? Within forty-eight hours, the researchers had caught and banded thirty-six owls, seventeen of which were the uncommon and evasive boreal owl. At that time, scientists thought the boreal owl was a rare northern species, one that had never been recorded in Michigan after the first of May. "The possibility that this banding success represented an annual spring nocturnal migration was stimulating enough to make owl banding an integral, if secondary, part of the overall project in subsequent years," wrote Alice Kelley and fellow owl researcher J. Roberts in a 1971 article about owl banding at the Point. Indeed, the discovery opened windows to research about owls at the Point and throughout the area. Before, little had been written about the owls, said Kelley. Likewise, little research had been done.

Kelley and Roberts visited the nets regularly throughout the night. They lived in a trailer at the site since only one motel many miles away was available. "At best," they wrote, "nights are cold on that windy point in April and May. Removing owls from nets by flashlight while avoiding needle-like talons is no task for the uninitiated."

Between 1966 and 1970, Alice Kelley and others banded 14 barred, 1 great gray, 129 long-eared, 1 short-eared, 39 boreal, and 280 northern saw-whet owls. Following Kelley came other owl banders: Art and Tom Carpenter and Bill Grigg, Lower Michigan dwellers who spent weekends, summers, and vacations in the UP. Like members of a secret society, they pitched tents and camped near the Point, banding owls and recording information as volunteers. These and other folks helped form the Whitefish Point Bird Observatory, which now hires researchers to band owls.

The findings of Carpenter, Grigg, and other owl banders led to theories that boreal owl populations are cyclical, falling and rising with some regularity. Terry P. Wiens showed evidence of the cyclical nature of boreal owls when comparing owl-banding data from Whitefish Point from 1978 to 1988. Low numbers occurred in all years except 1988, when 163 boreals were banded. During the fall of 1996, researchers again banded high numbers of boreal owls, adding more credence to the theory that this species irrupts once every nine or ten years. But Russell Utych thinks the data more clearly show a four-year irruption. Though the spring, 1997, owl-banding season was plagued with deep snow that remained into late April, banders caught seventy boreal owls, comparable to the highest seasons on record. In 1988 banders caught 152 boreal owls, in 1992 they caught 92 boreals, and in 1996 they caught 49.

Throughout the evening the banders work on study skins, talk, occasionally play cards or Chinese checkers, and ponder the world through midnight eyes. "At times, when you're walking out there, you see owls," says Susan Marden, tall, slender, and quiet, who also manages natural history data as a biologist in Tennessee. "At three in the morning, you're sure you see all kinds of owls. But they usually turn out to be tree stumps."

Other times, the owls are real. Once, a great gray owl hovered nearby while she walked the nets. Another time, a great gray sat in a tree watching Marden take a saw-whet owl from the net.

Owl-banding intern Mary Derr says seeing and banding her first owl, a tiny saw-whet, "was absolutely magical." Derr untangled it from the mist net, talked to it as she carried it through the woods, and banded it "all by myself." Owl bander Paul Dziepak recalls how one October day he "trudged from net to net every hour, listening to the saw-whet owl tape, trying to entice owls that apparently were not there." As he went to his final check, thinking about sleep, he noticed a ten-inch owl with large eyes looking at him, caught in the net—a boreal owl.

Later that season, he banded eleven boreal owls in one night.

Discovering a boreal owl in a net is a mystical experience. "Boreals are the devil owls. They fight you all the way," says Marden.

Exceedingly difficult to find, the boreal owl stands only ten inches tall and roosts deep within a conifer's branches, camouflaged to most humans. If you do discover this secretive species, you can identify it by its dark chocolate brown color, white-spotted head, and yellow beak and eyes. The boreal owl lives in North American coniferous forests as well as boreal forests in northern and central Europe and Asia. It preys mainly on voles but also on mice, shrews, gophers, squirrels, and chipmunks, as well as on songbirds and insects. This nomadic wanderer sometimes migrates south in winter to find food, but may return north to breed in summer, where the female selects a tree cavity in which to lay approximately six eggs, each about one to two days apart.

In March and April, birders listen for the primary courtship song of this owl, an eerie series of trills that can echo through the woods for several miles. Boreals also produce myriad other vocalizations such as murmurs, screeches, peeps, and moos.

Birders come to Whitefish Point envisioning the moment when they will add the rare boreal to their life list; most of them return unrewarded or having only seen the boreal at 6:30 A.M. on Saturday when a bander brings a specimen recently caught in the nets to show visitors. Birders do not add boreal owls to their life list if they have only seen it in a bander's hands.

When netted, the great gray owl and northern saw-whet remain complacent, docile, almost mellow. But the great horned and boreal owls are aggressive. "There's a real art to getting the boreal owl out of the net," says Jacob LaCroix. "You have to get the feet first and get them under control. Then come the shoulders, the body, and the head."

Feet. Shoulders. Body. Head. That is the owl bander's credo.

It is not the large, hooked bills of owls that can hurt banders if they are not careful, but rather the sharp, curved nails at the end of the long toes, which owls use to seize prey. But even if the owls seem fierce when caught in a mist net, they depend on humans to free them. The banders must constantly assess the bird's well-being when they're in the field. They must work quickly and note the owl's behavior. "If they're fighting against us, that's a good sign," says LaCroix.

One bander knew a long-eared owl was doing particularly well when it was caught just after dusk with a yellow-bellied sapsucker still bloodied in its mouth. Ornithologists named this owl species the long-eared because of the two tufts of feathers protruding from its head, which appear like ears. The owl raises and lowers the tufts to help camouflage itself. A roosting long-eared owl sits erect, narrows its body, and raises its tufts to look like broken tree branches. Slim and about sixteen inches long, this nocturnal bird looks like a large moth in flight as it hunts for mice, squirrels, chipmunks, and rabbits. It roosts by day in dense groves of cedars and pines in the north, and in palms in desert oases. A master of camouflage, it compresses its feathers close to its body so that it looks like a piece of bark on a tree limb. One day in late April, a group of birders walked through a boreal forest near the Point searching for a long-eared owl. Someone found one only after searching the ground for pellets, looking at pine tree after pine tree for whitewash, which indicates an owl's presence, and finally discovering one about twenty feet up in a pine tree sitting motionless on a branch.

The long-eared owl goes where the food and the habitat are. Instead of building a nest, the female, like many owl species, chooses an old squirrel or crow nest in a pine in which to lay her four to five oval, glossy white eggs. The young hatch within twenty-eight days. Both parents defend the young by screaming at intruders. By the time owl banders come to Whitefish Point, long-eared owls may be building nests here, but others are still moving, perhaps flying over the bay to nest in Canada.

The long-eared is the owl that banders look for from the dune just before they head to the nets. They go to the hawk dune at 8:30 P.M. and watch the sky for flying long-eared owls. Banders say that if a long-eared owl flies over the Point, at least one owl will fall into their nets later that night. Watching for this omen has become a ritual for them.

10 P.M. Round number two. The banders begin checking the nets again—same walk, same briskness, same shining of the light in the same spots.

No owls.

"Two nights in a row, we had what we thought was a perfect night, but no owls," says LaCroix. "The third day, there was a snowstorm. Perhaps they knew the storm was coming and were waiting it out. One night we saw twenty long-ears migrating over the dune at dusk. We caught eight long-ears that night. The next night we saw twenty-two owls on the dune and never caught one. You feel more tired when you don't catch any. But if there's even one bird, you don't feel tired at all."

During slow banding hours, the researchers can examine and update records. A northern saw-whet owl was banded on April 8, 1988, at Whitefish Point and then captured on October 4, 1988, at Cedar Grove in southeastern Wisconsin near the Lake Michigan shoreline. A saw-whet owl was seen on May 27, 1990, at Whitefish Point and again on November 11, 1990, at Cedar Grove. The banders know that a few related facts do not necessarily constitute a trend. Still, the information may be useful some day when studying the migratory habits of northern saw-whets.

Slightly larger than a robin, the northern saw-whet owl measures only seven inches tall. Its body is grayish red and it has a streaked white breast, lemon yellow eyes, and a black beak. The saw-whet nests in an abandoned woodpecker hole or other tree cavity in northern coniferous forests in the upper Great Lakes region, including the UP, as well as the western United States. It eats rodents, insects, and birds.

Rick Baetsen and Sue Andres have studied the nesting habits of northern saw-whet owls in the eastern and western parts of the UP. They, along with other researchers, survey the owl's nesting territories by playing a tape of their unique calls: monotonously repeated, single, high-pitched notes that sound like a toy train whistle. The researchers listen for a response, which means the northern saw-whet owl is defending territory. By analyzing their data, they have learned that this species prefers to breed in wet coniferous woods and upland pines in the UP, and that more saw-whets breed per square mile in the western part of the UP than in the eastern part.

11 P.M. Round three. No owls.

As midnight nears, the talk becomes more philosophical. "You have to like to travel, be open to doing this sort of thing," says LaCroix. "Yeah, and you never get tired of a job because you are never there long enough," says one researcher sitting on a table with two other nomadic souls who spend their Saturday nights partying with owls. They talk of other research adventures, of netting birds in the summers thick with biting black flies. "Your body builds up resistance," someone says. "You develop a tolerance to the insect saliva." No one really believes him, but it sounds plausible, and it's somehow reassuring tonight, when they still have not captured an owl.

The banders often tell stories about owls and magic, but not the type you would hear around a campfire. These are owl-banding stories. In 1988 the Whitefish Point Bird Observatory board raised enough money to hire its first staff owl bander, Peter Polisse. The Florida native used an alder branch that became known as the sacred push-stick or the bringer of owls to open the owl nets. That banding year was a big one: 260 owls were successfully banded and released. But the 1989 and 1990 seasons produced low numbers. Owl banders began to wonder why, until they learned that Polisse had taken the stick with him to Florida as a souvenir. They asked Polisse to return the stick. He did, and on March 31, 1991, banders ran the stick over the top of each net. The magical stick worked, says Steve Allen, a raptor-banding biologist that season. The first night the banders captured a saw-whet owl, and by the end of the first week they had banded six long-eared and six saw-whet owls.

Midnight. Round four.

Jacob LaCroix and Susan Marden walk methodically, never tripping, staying as close to the nets as possible without getting entangled, shining lights on each net from top to bottom. In the dark, they walk not hopeful, not pessimistic. Just looking for owls.

1 A.M. No owls.

2 A.M. No owls.

3 A.M. The first net. A huge owl is inside.

A great gray!

The silence of the still and chilled night air seems interrupted by the rapid pounding in the banders' hearts.

A great gray!

Quickly, LaCroix takes the great gray's feet. "A great gray!" he whispers over and over. The moment the owl is free from the net, LaCroix lifts it over his head and the bird tries to spreads its wide wings. "Isn't he beautiful?" LaCroix and Marden exclaim together. LaCroix carefully holds the wings and eases the massive bird, appearing to weigh much more than its two pounds, into a great gray owl-size coffee can.

The excitement of capturing this mysterious northern owl could easily overwhelm the banders. But they must continue the run. They must walk past ten more nets in twelve minutes. LaCroix holds onto the coffee can with the great gray owl inside and continues the same careful, prudent search through the obstacle course he has completed six times earlier that night.

Back at the station, Marden calls the hawk and waterbird counters, who had long gone to bed. "Come quickly," she says as LaCroix carefully prods the bird out of the coffee can. "We have a great gray."

They work swiftly inside the station to measure weight, wing extension, tail length, and other features. They find three generations of feathers on the bird, which means that it is at least three years old.

The great gray, with its round, tuftless head, large yellow eyes, and sooty gray plumage, is the largest North American owl. Its wings can spread to sixty inches. It stands twenty-two inches tall. The great horned owl is smaller, with a wingspan of over forty-eight inches and a height of twenty inches, but it weighs more than the great gray does. While the great horned easily adapts to many habitats throughout North America because of its eclectic diet, the great gray owl has a more specialized diet of snowshoe hares, shrews, squirrels, and other mammals, and that makes finding prey more difficult. Snow may be falling when the female great horned owl is incubating her eggs in the UP, but the great gray is still desperately searching for food to make it through the winter. The birds are often so hungry that they plunge right in front of humans into a crusty, snow-packed field to secure a mouse. A great gray can detect a rodent beneath the snow by sound and catches it with a swift, silent plunge-dive. If snow is topped with crusty ice, it makes it difficult for the great gray to catch its prey. This spectacular bird can starve to death during bad winters, even though its large size makes it seem invincible. The first-born of the season is especially vulnerable as winter conditions linger.

Most frequently seen in the boreal climatic zones of North America and Eurasia, the great gray ventures farther south in winter when prey is not plentiful in its usual haunts. Observers document several great grays each year in Michigan's eastern UP, especially near Whitefish Point and Sault Ste. Marie.

The male calls his low, haunting, *hoo-hoo-hooo* to attract a mate, who lays two to three eggs in an abandoned hawk, crow, or eagle nest. Great grays prefer to nest in spruce and pine forests near swamps or clearings. The male hunts mainly in the dark over open bogs and wet meadows near the nest. He feeds the female, who stays with the young, brooding them for about twenty-one to twenty-eight days. The young then move around the nest tree, peering out from a branch, then retreating to the nest when alarmed. The adults teach them to hunt, and when they are able to catch prey on their own, the young fly off into the forests to find their own hunting territories.

Whitefish Point Bird Observatory conducted a radiotelemetry study of great gray owls for several years to track the nesting habits of the species, which breeds in tamarack bogs in Manitoba as well as meadows among coniferous forests in Oregon and pine/fir forests in California. But do great grays breed in Michigan? Biologists guess that they do, but no proof exists. Research has shown that great grays will use artificial, human-made nesting platforms. To attract great grays, biologists recently placed large nesting platforms in select trees in Lake Superior State Forest and Tahquamenon Falls State Park, ten miles south of Whitefish Point. They also radio-tagged four adult females. In summer 1992, a researcher followed a female great gray via the radio monitoring program. She remained in a spruce–tamarack bog near the Tahquamenon River from June 2 through August 10. The bird was seen four times, and according to Gregory Fischer, one of the principal investigators in this project, "on every visual inspection, the owl was either hunting or resting and showed no signs of stress." No nesting was reported for this or any other great gray owl in Michigan. Should a great gray female be found on a nest, history will be made, relevant management strategies can be implemented, and knowledge of this species will grow. But scientists rely heavily on funding—the project begins, then gets interrupted, then begins again. In 1994, funding problems stalled the radiotelemetry project. No one knows if it will begin again.

Whitefish Point researchers have also banded great grays in the area during winter, and in 1992 they had the chance to closely observe this beautiful, mysterious creature. Great grays were staging a record winter invasion near Sault Ste. Marie, fifty miles away from the Point. Great grays perched everywhere in downtown Sault Ste. Marie—on buildings, on telephone posts. At times, people could see eight at a time. One observer saw fifteen great grays along the ravines on Sugar Island. Researchers banded thirty-nine different great grays within a fifty-mile radius in the winter of 1991–92.

Banders particularly understand the fragility of the great gray when they remove it from the net. It remains complacent, allowing banders to weigh it and measure its tail length and wing chords. The awe that struck Jacob LaCroix when he first saw the great gray in the net is now replaced with a sense of purpose and duty. He must quickly gather the data so that the bird can be released unharmed and sent back on its journey.

LaCroix takes the still and silent bird outdoors. He sets it on the ground, pauses for a moment, then walks backward slowly.

The owl hops once, twice. Then it flies.

Quiet, powerful wings beat gracefully into what seems to us another dimension, where it will join its brethren, the gods and goddesses of the night that are flying across the Point.

Common Loon

Secrets of the Northern Diver

M INK FROGS CROAK IN THE MARSHES and deep pools of Ottawa National Forest near Watersmeet, Michigan. As twilight tapers to darkness, David Evers tug-starts a motor on a boat, then aims for an island where a loon chick was born four weeks ago. He and three other researchers approach the loon's nest site. He slows the motor, then stops it.

The boat drifts into the silence, sending ripples across the lake.

A-A-WHOO-QUEE-QUEE. WHEOO-QUEE.

A-A-WHOO-QUEE-QUEE. WHEOO-QUEE.

An adult male common loon approaches to investigate the intruder, actually a taped recording of a loon wail.

The human spotlighter shines one million candlepower in the loon's red eye. The loon moves to within thirty feet. Evers peeps like a newborn loon, an irresistible call to an adult caring for young. The loon swims closer to the sound, and when it gets close enough, Evers instantly reaches to net the adult. Quickly and adeptly, the researchers band and weigh the bird, determine its sex, take a blood sample, and snip two feathers. Within minutes, they return the loon to the wild.

Using the innovative technique of imitating a newborn chick's peeping to capture and band loons, these researchers have collected information that has changed forever the way humans view loons. Ten years of data are negating loon myths and offering insight on how mercury affects fish-eating birds, and, perhaps, even humans. Contrary to romantic belief, the common loon does not necessarily mate for life. Although a loon remains faithful to its chosen lake, returning north year after year to its nesting lands, this thick-billed bird with iridescent black head, piercing red eyes, and black-and-white checkerboard back often changes mates in the middle of the nesting season for reasons biologists are just beginning to explore. Evers and other UP researchers as well as those in other parts of the country are earnestly learning all they can about this species, which has lived on Earth for at least 60 million years. The loon's future, however, remains uncertain as humans deposit pesticides, oil, and other chemicals into the waters where the bird feeds, and disturb the once-remote islands where it breeds and the deep lakes and oceans where it spends winters.

Five species of loons exist in North America: the Arctic, the Pacific, the common, the red-throated, and the yellow-billed. The red-throated, Arctic, Pacific, and yellow-billed breed in northwestern Canada and winter along the Pacific Coast. The common loon, whose yodels are a symbol of the remote north woods, winters on the Atlantic and Pacific Coasts of North America, from Newfoundland to southern Florida and from the western Aleutian Islands to Baja California and the Pacific Coast of Mexico. When breeding season comes, the common loon raises its young in Alaska, Canada, Greenland, and Iceland; parts of Montana, Idaho, and Washington; New England; and the Great Lake states of Michigan, Wisconsin, and Minnesota. The common loon once nested as far south as Iowa, Illinois, Indiana, Ohio, Pennsylvania, and California, but habitat loss and other problems have extirpated the bird from those states. In Michigan and several other states, the loon is designated as threatened or a species of special concern.

Michigan's UP continues to offer nesting habitat for loons and in turn, a place for humans to study the species during breeding season. Ottawa and Hiawatha National Forests contain excellent loon breeding habitat—deep freshwater lakes well stocked with fish and with undisturbed islands where loons build their nests. The Ottawa Forest's Watersmeet District, just north of Wisconsin in the southwestern UP, harbors one of the highest densities of nesting common loons in Michigan. Isle Royale National Park, a group of islands in Lake Superior north of the UP, also provides the isolation loons require in the form of long, protected coves along the Lake Superior shoreline. Some sixty nesting pairs of loons inhabit the inland lakes and Lake Superior shoreline in summer. In addition, marshes and deep pools at Seney National Wildlife Refuge, in the middle of the UP, are managed to attract nesting loons and other wild creatures.

David Evers and his three partners operate the not-for-profit BioDiversity Research Institute, now headquartered in Maine, that gains financial support for and guides loon research throughout most of its breeding and wintering range in the United States. The partners are Joe Kaplan, a defender of loons who leads the Michigan and midwestern work; Jim Paruk, a talkative tree specialist and biologist who works with a volunteer loon-study program for Earthwatch; and Pete Reaman, a Maine native who met Evers at Whitefish Point Bird Observatory in the northeastern UP in 1990. Evers directed the organization while Reaman, then a young biologist recently graduated from college, counted waterfowl and banded owls. Today they work with organizations such as the North American Loon Fund, the Canadian Lakes Loon survey, and the Michigan Loon Preservation Association.

Reaman admits he sometimes wonders why he's not working someplace else making more money. But he knows the answer to that question is in his heart. "It's important *how* you make your money," he says. "Too often people want to just make money. People need to find good, fulfilling work."

Evers found good, fulfilling work in a log cabin off a quiet, single-lane road that cut through bog and forest on its way to the end of Whitefish Point in the UP. "The research on the Upper Peninsula's loon population, particularly at the Seney National Wildlife Refuge, provides us with information available nowhere else," says Evers. Of medium height and dark haired, Evers speaks with a warm, earnest voice and alive, concerned eyes. Evers embraces a longtime friend with the same affection he strokes a loon's feathers. "Financial security doesn't come with the territory," he says. "But then there's never any guarantee whatever you do. So you just make sure you have other options."

"I've always had a propensity to work for nonprofits," adds the Lake Superior State College graduate now working on a doctoral degree at the University of Minnesota. "I'm a cause-oriented person. I want to make a difference," he says. And he doesn't want to have to work for someone else to do that. "I'm independent and I want to be creative."

Those personality traits emerged when Evers began studying loons in the 1980s. At that time, scientists could not confidently say how much the identically plumaged male and female common loon shared in egg incubation. Do they return to the same spot to reproduce? Do their offspring return to the same place? Do they really mate for life? And why do some loons choose more than one lake for their territory? Is it because they need to find more food?

That type of information is known with certainty about many avian species, but it wasn't known about loons, a bird that has captured the imagination of so many for so long. In the past few decades, scientists have been trying to answer these questions as well as why loons are declining in some of their historical North American breeding range.

One way to find answers is by banding birds. But the common loon has never been an easy bird to catch and band. Successful banding has been done, but the catches have been sporadic, lucky strikes. Evers didn't know the difficulties of banding loons when he decided to research the great diver of the north. But he did know that the loon was in jeopardy, and he wanted to find out why. Only about three hundred pairs of common loons bred in Michigan in the 1980s, and those were confined to the northern part of the state. Yet at the turn of the twentieth century, hundreds to thousands of pairs nested statewide. The common loon remained on Michigan's threatened list in 1999, though attempts have been made to delist it. Scientists have attributed the common loon's decline to habitat destruction, breeding-habitat disturbance, and fish contamination.

Loons need isolated islands in lakes large enough for them to take flight. If a loon lands on a lake that is not large enough for takeoff, the bird could become stranded and perish. The loon's legs and large, webbed feet are situated far back on its body, making walking on land difficult. Yet the loon can almost walk on water as it takes flight, like a plane gathering speed on the runway before becoming airborne. While clumsy on land, a loon is so agile in water that it can thrust its body forward into a deep dive to snatch minnows, pike, perch, gizzard shad, crappies, bullheads, and other fish. A loon can remain submerged for ninety seconds, regenerating its oxygen supply in a way scientists don't fully understand. And it can swim faster than a brook trout, one of its favorite meals. Loons will not breed if they cannot find a sufficient food source, and they require privacy; motorized boats on a lake drive them away. Humans, it seems, are making life extremely difficult for loons.

Jim Kessel, a former biologist at Seney National Wildlife Refuge, was also searching for a way to consistently band loons when Evers began work on his master's thesis in the 1980s. They worked together to find a more dependable loon-banding technique. "In the past, banders worked against the loons instead of with them," says Evers. "They went out in scuba gear with large nets and decoys to overwhelm a loon. As soon as the loon came to the decoy, they'd bring the net in on poles from underneath the water to catch the loon. It didn't work." A loon can dive to depths of two hundred feet, emerging in a place far from where it went underwater, leading the bewildered scientist on a wild loon chase. Obviously, speeding around a large lake in a motorboat to track loons was not going to work, nor was it the most humane approach. These banders were doing admirable jobs, the best they could do with the knowledge they had, but they kept searching for a more productive way to band loons.

"What I discovered was actually a culmination of what others have learned over the years," Evers says. "Everything was trial and error, putting together what others had tried before and picking out the pieces of the puzzle that worked." For instance, a loon dives straight forward, but banders often tried to catch the bird from behind. By the time the researchers extended the net, the loon was long gone. "We missed a lot of loons trying to capture them from behind. One day, we thought, why not put the net out in front of the loon, so as it moves forward to dive it will head right into the net?" That solved, they set out to discover how they could make consistent, successful captures. The answer came from considering what birders do on Christmas bird counts to attract owls—they play tape recordings of the call of the owl. Evers thought, why not play a recording of the loon's call to lure the loons closer?

In summer, a loon's vocalizations are a magical sound—but the loons are not talking to people, they are talking to one another. To defend its territory or when it is disturbed by predators, humans, or other intruders, the loon utters a laughing tremolo of varying intensity and length.

The loon sings its tremolo on land or water or when flying. Sometimes the loon combines the tremolo with a yodel, the most complex loon vocalization. Given by the male, a yodel consists of a slowly rising note, followed by several phrases of rising and falling pitches. A loon yodels to defend and identify its territory. A tremolo-yodel may signal a loon's anxiety about possible intruders as well as its desire to defend its territory. A loon also makes quiet, intimate, one-syllable hoots to maintain contact with its mate or chicks.

The most frequently heard loon call, the wail, rises in pitch like a clarinet playing a scale. A loon utters its haunting wail with its mouth closed, perhaps to amplify the sound. At night, one loon may begin a wave of wails that echoes for miles. Other loons may join in, adding their yodels and tremolos to the chorus.

Often when a loon hears a wail, it swims closer to the sound to investigate. That knowledge has led scientists to play tapes of loon wails to get the bird to come close enough to the boat to net and band it. But a loon responding to a wail call "will only come so close, to within twenty to thirty feet, and often that's not close enough to catch the loon for banding," says Evers.

The penultimate night of his first summer studying loons, Evers sat in the boat at midnight, tired and frustrated. His project was not going well. He had not banded any loons. He played the wail call and observed the loon get closer, just as he had done other times that summer and just as many other loon researchers had done before him. But then Evers heard something that gave him an idea. A chick was calling softly, peenting, ostensibly to a parent nearby. Instinctively, Evers tried to imitate the chick. The adult moved so close to Evers that he was able to capture and band it. He then set it back into the water so it could resume its parental duties. Using this new technique, Evers captured five loons for his graduate research project in the late 1980s at Seney.

The following summer, even though his graduate thesis work was done, he felt compelled to return to see if the loons he banded would return to breed. He longed to hear the tremolos, yodels, and wails of the magical bird with a nearly six-foot wingspread. He longed to inhale the fresh, sweet UP summer air. He wanted to experience once again the thrill of observing the loon chicks hitch a ride on their parents' backs and learn to swim, dive, and catch their own food. And to laugh when the young insisted their parents feed them fish, crustaceans, and plants long after they were ready to fend for themselves.

The five banded loons did return to Seney that next year. They built their nests of grasses and twigs upon which they laid one to three eggs, then settled down to keep the eggs warm and wait for the time, in about thirty days, when they would hatch. As the loon chicks hatched, so did the beginning of Evers's life working with loons. Soon he expanded his project to Ottawa and Hiawatha National Forests, Isle Royale National Park, and a three-county area in north-central Wisconsin. He hired researchers, and they began to study loons in even greater earnest.

The researchers fit the birds with two or three different colored bands, which provide more than one thousand possible combinations, enough to readily identify each loon. Once the birds are banded, the researchers can observe loon behavior and record data. The researchers spend hundreds of hours in Upper Michigan, Minnesota, Wisconsin, Maine, Alaska, and other states and provinces during the breeding season, taking and evaluating blood samples from adults and even yolk samples from eggs, and observing loons in time activity budgets.

Time activity budgets involve observing a loon's every action or inaction for a predetermined amount of time: four, eight, or more hours. A researcher doing time-activity budgets may sit in a boat on a hot summer day for hours as a loon incubates its eggs. A breeze on the lake helps keep away the swarm of bugs back on land. Or a researcher might prop himself against a tree on an island and sit quietly, watching a loon be a loon. Some days, nothing happens, and a researcher can wonder what possessed him to sit still for four hours enduring boredom. Other times it can be a meditative experience, in which the quiet wilderness lulls the observer into another dimension. But awareness is paramount. Every single movement a loon makes must be recorded on a data sheet. If the loon turns around on its nest, the researcher records the action. Three and a half minutes of preening. Sixty-five minutes of stillness. Don't doze off, because suddenly the loon will engage in two minutes of foot waggling. During a waggle, a loon raises one foot in the air, holds it for a few seconds, and then shakes it loosely. Afterwards, the loon dips its foot in the water and repeats the waggle. Foot waggling probably helps maintain a loon's body temperature. Chicks, whose small bodies tend to heat and cool more quickly than those of the larger-bodied adults, waggle their feet three times more often than adults. Adults also foot-waggle three times more often during July than in May, and July is one of the warmest months in the UP. How do scientists know the frequency of foot waggling? By reviewing the reams of data they gathered. Sitting hunched over a computer with data sheets spread helter-skelter, researchers sometimes wish they were back out on the boat with the hot sun blasting them instead of fighting to keep their eyes focused on numbers. They know, however, that countless hours recording loon behavior can lead to a new insight, one that might help save the loon.

"It was always thought that common loons are lifetime mates and that they won't find another mate unless theirs perishes," says Evers. "It's a nice thought, but we are finding that's not always true." For example, a female banded in 1989 had spent two consecutive summers on a deep pond called D-Pool at Seney National Wildlife Refuge. In 1990, Kaplan banded her mate. In 1991, the female returned to D-Pool and paired with an unbanded male. Nothing unusual about that; perhaps her first mate had died. But then, researchers discovered the banded male, her mate from the previous year, in a nearby territory. The next year, the banded female paired with her original mate.

"The nest failed, and two days later, he's gone, and an unbanded male is in there to take his place. We are thinking this is most likely a reproductive strategy." Switching mates frequently happens with both sexes, although more so with females. About half of the loons the researchers observed renested if the first attempt failed. Frequently, they watched a trio of a female and two males perform circle dances until the female and one male chased away the other male. This behavior, called rapid mate switching, is possibly triggered by nest failure.

At least 20 percent of the loons BioDiversity researchers surveyed for five years switched mates annually. Scientists are beginning to discover that more of the world's avian species than they had thought change mates suddenly during nesting season. "Rapid mate switching can include two females and a male," adds Keren Tischler, who works with Joe

Kaplan studying the Michigan loons. "It can also happen early in the season in addition to after a nest failure."

"We also found out that loons switch lakes as often as they switch mates," says Kaplan.

But the question weighs heavily on their minds: Is rapid mate switching a natural reproductive strategy for loons, or is there a link between mate switching and pollution?

To find the answer, scientists are testing the levels of mercury in live, healthy loons. The researchers take blood samples and snip two feathers from which they can later measure mercury levels. Mercury tends to concentrate in a loon's feathers. Back at the laboratory, they place the two feathers in an acid solution that breaks down the feathers, enabling scientists to analyze mercury content. In the past few years, researchers have found elevated levels of mercury in 25 percent of the breeding adult populations of loons they studied. Is it coincidence that a little less than 25 percent of the loons they observed also engaged in rapid mate switching?

Most mercury gets into lake systems from atmospheric deposition. Industrial coal-burning, incineration, and other processes pollute the air. This pollution can travel for hundreds of miles, falling on lakes where loons breed. When the mercury falls into the water, bacteria convert it to an organic form called methylmercury. Fish ingest the methylmercury, then pass it on to loons that eat the fish. As the methylmercury makes its way up the food chain, it concentrates within each higher predator. Research has shown that mercury levels in Minnesota and Wisconsin have increased by 400 percent during the past one hundred fifty years.

Loons don't normally directly die from mercury poisoning. But high levels of mercury in their systems can make them more susceptible to disease and slow their response to external stimuli such as an approaching predator. One Michigan-captured male loon with above-normal mercury levels would not incubate the eggs laid by its mate. Normally males share equally in that responsibility or at least help when the female leaves the nest to feed. The nest failed. The male was found later that summer, dead. "The cause of death was unquestionably due to mercury poisoning," says Evers. "We recorded over forty parts per million in the loon's feather." That's four times the normal amount. It is just one example, but it does suggest the possibility that high mercury levels are severely affecting loon reproductive behavior. And the information mirrors data gathered in the 1970s by Canadian Wildlife Service biologist Jack Barr, who found that loons with two to three parts per million of methylmercury in their brain tissues nested less frequently than loons with lower or no amounts of the substance. In addition, the loons with the higher amounts of methylmercury also tended their nests less and defended their territories less.

Back then, Barr worked with dead loons to gather information on mercury poisoning. Now that researchers have discovered better banding methods, they can gather the data on live loons. "Recapture is the key aspect in getting mercury samples," says Kaplan. "You recapture birds year after year and patterns emerge. For instance, we've found a correlation between pH levels and mercury levels. With low pH and high acid we found higher methylmercury content. This is what the project is all about, what conditions cause mercury loading in loons? This is a good way to monitor if there's a problem."

Complicating the studies is the fact that mercury is found in the natural environment and that not all scientists agree on the mercury-loon connection or how it works. Researcher Lawrence Alexander attributed a large number of loon deaths in Florida in the late 1980s to mercury poisoning. He said mercury in the loons' systems made them weak and unable to catch their favored prey, fish. Instead they ate blue crabs, from which they contracted parasites that ate away at their stomachs. Alexander died before his theory could be proven. While agreeing that loon numbers are down, some scientists say the tie-in between eating crabs and mercury levels does not exist. Most scientists today believe that loons are sensitive to mercury and are one of the better indicators of how harmful this chemical can be.

Loon research now includes examining the amount of mercury in bodies of water throughout upper North America. A geographic trend is emerging. The level of mercury is higher in the eastern than in the western part of the United States. Loons in Alaska have low levels of mercury, only about 0.5 parts per million. In the Great Lakes, loons average 1.1 parts per million, and in New England, the number rises to 2.3 parts per million. The data support the theory that westerly winds carry mercury from power plants, incinerators, and other sources nationwide.

What does this research mean for humans? Loons eat fish contaminated with mercury. So do humans. And some studies suggest unborn fetuses subjected to certain amounts of mercury may suffer development problems. High doses of methylmercury can cause mental retardation and kidney damage. Hundreds of Japanese in the mid 1950s became ill or died after eating mercury-contaminated seafood. During a famine in the early 1970s, Iraqis ate seed grain coated with methylmercury, which was used as a fungicide. More than 450 people died, and more than 6,500 others suffered neurological problems. The findings are provocative enough for state and federal governments to watch as the results of these studies unfold. BioDiversity's Pete Reaman carefully adds that some studies negate one another, and that is another reason why loon researchers must continue their work.

Mercury is not the only potential hazard for loons. Lead poisoning and habitat destruction are also culprits. Recent statistics suggest loon deaths in eighteen states, including Michigan and Wisconsin, can be attributed to lead poisoning from fishing sinkers. As a result, the U.S. Environmental Protection Agency is contemplating regulating the use of lead in fishing tackle and researching nontoxic alternatives. Other causes of death include colliding with boat propellers or getting entangled in fishing lines.

As people flock to remote lakes where loons nest, the loons leave. Loons simply do not want to nest near humans. Some states have recognized these facts and are educating the public about what conditions loons need to successfully reproduce. New Hampshire, for example, is preserving loon habitat and roping loon breeding territories so that humans will not intrude. Pete Reaman hopes Michigan will do the same.

At Isle Royale National Park, park staff and researchers have been recording loon reproductive success since 1989, both for Lake Superior and inland lake waters. Isle Royale harbors the only known loon population that uses Great Lakes waters for nesting; the protected bays and islands around the park serve as critical habitat for loons. This 45-mile-long archipelago encompasses 850 square miles including submerged lands that extend four miles into Lake Superior. The group of islands are numerous parallel ridges of ancient lava flows that were tilted and glaciated. For now, Isle Royale, a United States Biosphere Reserve, remains relatively untouched by outside influences. "The region serves as a control site for what loons have done for thousands of years in a system not burdened by contaminants and human disturbance," says Joe Kaplan.

He recently met Michael Meetz and William Beckman, two volunteers and longtime friends who have canoed the inland lakes and Lake Superior shoreline around Isle Royale to count loon chicks each summer since 1991. Paddling the clear waters, Meetz and Beckman hear howling wolves and see moose running along the rugged shoreline. The weather changes constantly; a day that begins sunny can, within minutes, change to a stormy, windy scene.

And they love it. "That's my vacation," says Meetz, a scientist from Nevada, Iowa. He and his friend Beckman, a junior-high school geography teacher and resident of Maple Grove, Minnesota, have canoed and hiked together for years, though raising families and moving to different towns sometimes made it difficult for them to plan outings. When Meetz learned the National Park Service was looking for volunteers to count loon chicks at Isle Royale, he called Beckman, and they began their yearly venture of enjoying the wilderness together.

"The terrain is rough." says Meetz. "It's virtually untouched except for the trails. You have to be willing to stay in a cabin or in a tent, then hike and boat out onto a lake." In some places, they follow moose trails with a compass. "I've gotten confused out there," says Meetz, "but never lost."

Meetz and Beckman count chicks in August when they are seven to nine weeks old. It's an interesting time in the loon's reproductive stage. The chicks are old enough to swim and investigate new territory, yet young enough to be protected by their parents, who continue territorial displays and vocalizations much to the delight of Meetz and Beckman. Counting chicks isn't always easy, however, because when the young detect an intruder, they flatten themselves against the water or slip into the reeds. "When you're in a canoe, the chicks spot you quickly," Meetz says. "We try to walk along the shore to count them or remain in a designated campsite and just sit and watch the loons until sunset. Your senses just come alive out there," he says. "Your sight, your hearing. Even your smell. You regain some of those things you lose." Returning to civilization after being out in the wilderness for several weeks can be so disconcerting, he adds, that having to look both ways before crossing a street becomes a major chore.

In the ten years he and Beckman have been counting chicks, Meetz has seen high and low population fluctuations and wonders if that's a normal loon reproduction cycle. "What's important," he says, "is that we do a long-term comparison of numbers." That's why he and Beckman want to continue counting loon chicks each summer.

In 1996 and 1997, Meetz and Beckman recorded only fifteen and twenty loon chicks that survived through August. In 1998, Meetz and Beckman, along with additional help from Kaplan and Keren Tischler, recorded forty-one chicks that likely survived into August. The researchers surveyed forty-seven of the Island's interior lakes and thirty-three locations along the Lake Superior shoreline. Kaplan says chick productivity has been low at Isle Royale, but the reasons remain unclear.

"Ongoing monitoring is also showing us how vulnerable loons are to human disturbance, especially during the critical nesting period (late April to early July). Loons will not tolerate humans coming close to their nests," says Kaplan. "Since 1997, we are aware of at least three situations where boating activity—both powerboats and paddlers—have contributed to the abandonment of nests or the loss of a chick because they passed too close to a nest or a family with young."

The park's natural resource management staff has begun working on loon education projects to teach visitors how to cause less disturbance to the loons. Meetz says that whenever he and Beckman travel between Isle Royale and the mainland, a six-hour boat trip, they offer their fellow travelers a ten-minute talk on the loon to help people understand the need to protect this bird's habitat.

Meanwhile, Kaplan says initial research at Isle Royale and other places in the UP shows more than ever how complicated the mercury contamination process is. "We banded nine-week-old chicks and found a range of 0.61 parts per million to 15.3 parts per million in their feathers," he says. "We can find a chick with 0.5 parts per million in one lake and another chick in a lake right next door with 10 parts per million." That's probably because each lake's chemistry is different and reacts differently to atmospheric deposition of mercury. More education, more research, and more knowledge can only help ensure the survival of the common loon. Kaplan says the biologists have also fine-tuned their loon capture techniques so they can band nonbreeding birds. That will help them gather even more clues about the relationship between mercury levels, loon reproduction, and population declines.

Activist organizations are also making sure that the loon is not delisted from the Michigan threatened species list until certain goals have been met. When the Michigan Department of Natural Resources called for downlisting the birds to special concern status in 1998, members of the Loon Preservation Association and its Loon Watch program vehemently opposed the action. Approximately 1,200 loons now live in Michigan during breeding season, but that's still short of the goal of 570 to 575 breeding pairs.

Luckily for the loons, researchers remain loyal to the yodelers of the north. "Loons are so compelling," says Peg Hart, who also has worked with loons in Michigan. "Loons are so cognizant, so aware. They are not like any other waterfowl. They see an eagle coming from a mile away. It is almost as if they have a thought process." Although attributing human characteristics to birds is often taboo in the research world, Hart can't help adding that she can actually see expressions on loons' faces. "Loons hear and see you before you get to the lake," she says. "That makes them interesting to watch. I come up in a boat and I know right away whether the loon has a mate on the nest. You can see the loon sitting on the shore, and it looks askance. They're stoic. You go out on a lake into their territory and they'll be far apart. The pair will join to investigate the intruder together. Loons know the difference between an osprey and an eagle. If you hear a loon wail, you often look up and see an eagle." An eagle is a threat because it may prey on loon chicks, but osprey eat fish and are less threatening.

Even David Evers, who has worked in the field for fifteen years now, writing report after report, calling foundation after foundation to secure grants, remains enamored with the common loon. "After watching loons for hundreds of hours, day after day, I still don't tire of it," he says. "Loons are addictive. Most everyone who works with us ends up addicted to loons."

That addiction may be what compels humans to discover more secrets about a bird whose nighttime wail has rung across the UP's lakes for thousands of years, and whose survival could depend on the people who listen to its song.

Yellow Rail

Night of the Yellow Rail

IT IS JUNE 20 AND NEARLY 10 P.M. at Seney National Wildlife Refuge. A great blue heron can still see well enough to fly over a marsh. The air is muggy, downright hot for this time of year. Pink clouds, still heavy with the sun's latent light, float in a grayish sky.

It is not time yet. It must be completely dark.

Impregnating the air is a scent that can only be experienced on the first full day of summer, a day when twenty-four hours of sunlight shine on the Arctic Circle and almost as many shine on the UP. It is a reminiscent, ephemeral smell, like Grandma's chicken soup simmering in a pot.

At the Seney refuge on this longest day of the year, two loons flap wings. One yodels, then dives underwater, followed by the other. An immature eagle, nearly the size of an adult, sits on its nest. The parent perches on a tree nearby. Four cygnet swans squeak softly, following the parent trumpeter swan into the penumbra. A common snipe, one hundred feet in the air, swoops to earth, its vibrating tail feathers creating an eerie whistle.

Even as it gets so dark that a human cannot see the swarm of mosquitos buzzing inches away, the sounds of snipes merge with the voices of the night. Mink frogs rumble like horses' hooves on cobblestones while spring peepers, tiny woodland frogs the size of a thumb, repeat soft, high, sleighbell-like pitches.

At midnight, Seney biologist Richard Urbanek and two of his interns, feet embedded in waders and jeans stained with mucky sedge slime, drive the back roads of the ninety-six-thousand-acre wildlife refuge. They bounce in their van down the marsh-matted road. They know exactly where to stop. They unload and head into the night, carrying flashlights, nets, and two small rocks less than an inch thick, several inches long, and an inch wide.

Urbanek stands at the edge of a wet meadow where a mat-forming sedge dominates. A few willows grow at the habitat's perimeter, their loose, carefree branches swaying amid the top of the wet sedges.

Kick Kick Kickee Kick.

Urbanek taps the rocks together, then waits.

Kick Kick Kickee Kick.

The percussive sound resonates.

Marsh wrens, sounding like clattering typewriters, chatter from a hidden spot within the cattails while sedge wrens call their crisper, percussive notes from somewhat drier areas. A porcupine munches peacefully on tender, young leaves, while balancing itself, using its bristly tail, on a three-foot-tall shrub.

Urbanek is not listening for wrens or looking for porcupines. He is listening for the yellow rail, one of the most secretive birds in the world, to answer the rocks with its clicking mating call. But no yellow rail calls tonight.

Urbanek, awake for nearly the past twenty-four hours, is covered with painful welts from the black flies that bit him while he counted songbirds in the woods at 5 A.M. Still, he chooses to remain awake, continuing to tap the rocks, hoping to hear the rail he has banded and studied for nearly two decades at Seney. Breeding season in the UP requires a twenty-four-hour-per-day commitment from biologists like Urbanek. If he appears a bit unkempt—his hair uncombed, his shirt a tad wrinkled—that is because he has more important things to do in June than worry about appearances.

Urbanek, a bachelor, admits life can be lonely for a biologist living in one of the last North American wildernesses, alone in a small house where the winters are long, quiet, and solitary. Then in spring and summer when the tourists come, Urbanek is so busy working, banding Kirtland's warblers in Lower Michigan, doing breeding-bird surveys in the UP, and leading yellow rail tours that he barely gets three or four hours of sleep each night, let alone any free night to socialize. Urbanek muses that he studied wildlife as an alternative to working on the family farm back in southern Illinois, but his hours seem to resemble those of a farmer. Growing up in Pinckneyville, Illinois, in a family of nine, Urbanek watched his parents work hard, barely making enough to feed the family. "We were so poor," he says, "that I didn't own a pair of binoculars." But he had his mind and his feet—so he went romping through the southern Illinois countryside, wading through streams and hiking the rolling hills. It was rural, wild, and free.

As for his decision to earn a bachelor's and a master's degree in zoology at Southern Illinois University, Urbanek says, "I knew I was going to work in wildlife for as long as I could think."

When Urbanek went to Ohio State University to get his doctorate in zoology, he discovered one of nature's most secretive birds. In 1981, Urbanek's professor, Theodore A. Bookhout, took him to a place he had never been before, Seney National Wildlife Refuge. There he showed Urbanek a bird as quirky as the man who now studies it.

Urbanek was drawn to this wild place where "you go out in the middle of the night and tap two rocks together and the yellow rail comes out." He found it intriguing that this bird makes such an unusual call, that it responds so readily to man-made sounds, and that ornithologists knew so little about the it—true even today. What was known of this rare rail was limited to descriptions of the male's territorial call and, to a lesser degree, the bird's breeding habitat. Growing interest in birds in the 1970s spawned more scientific research on the species. Bookhout was one of the first to start yellow rail research at Seney. His students, including Stenzel and Urbanek, followed in his wading-boot footsteps. That first experience was enough to keep Urbanek at the wildlife refuge ever since, working summers since 1981 and living here permanently since 1991.

Bookhout also introduced Urbanek to another unique research project, trying to prove that the federally endangered whooping crane could be reintroduced into places where it once bred. Bookhout and Urbanek collected sandhill crane eggs in mid-May from Seney, Lake Superior State Forest, and Hiawatha National Forest, then reared the chicks in a hatchery. Urbanek lived nearby in a trailer to tend to the chicks. Sandhill crane chicks readily attach to the first voice they hear or the first living animal they see, so humans did not talk in front of the chicks, and they fed the chicks using a puppet that looks like a crane.

When it came time to release color-banded chicks in late August and early September, Urbanek followed them to see if they would migrate with their wild brethren. They did, flying first to Jasper-Pulaski National Wildlife Refuge in Indiana, a major stopover for thousands of sandhill cranes, and then flying to their wintering grounds in Georgia and Florida. The theory was that if that could be done with sandhill cranes, it could be done with whooping cranes. The hope is that this technique can be used to reintroduce self-sustaining populations of endangered whooping cranes at Seney National Wildlife Refuge. Today, that hope is still just a hope, although Urbanek says sometime in the beginning of the twenty-first century he may be involved in a whooping crane reintroduction project in either Canada, Minnesota, Wisconsin, or perhaps at Seney. Urbanek hopes to be a part of the team that reintroduces the cranes.

For now Urbanek focuses his work on yellow rails, one of the wildest, most elusive creatures at Seney. And though he misses companionship some days, Urbanek has never stopped loving the wildness of Seney. "This is still the neatest place I've seen," he says. "This is about as wild as you can get in the Midwest. There's a high proportion of wild habitat to people."

The yellow rail seems to enjoy the same quiet, mysterious solitude that Urbanek does. Only a short window of opportunity exists for humans to encounter and study this shy, sparrow-sized bird with a short, maize yellow bill and dark stripes on a yellowish brown back. For several weeks in late spring, in the middle of the night, the male yellow rail makes its unusual clicking, rhythmic calls in the Seney marshes to deter other suitors. Through twenty years of research during these otherworldly hours, Urbanek and his fellow biologists have made some remarkable discoveries regarding site fidelity and breeding practices of this species.

Birders lust after yellow rails. Ornithologists know little about the bird's habitat, nesting requirements, breeding population densities, or behavior on the breeding grounds. "The yellow rail is extremely difficult to observe because of its secretive habits, its reluctance to fly, and its preference for remote areas," wrote Jeffrey R. Stenzel in *Ecology of Breeding Yellow Rails at Seney National Wildlife Refuge.* Stenzel, a student of Bookhout's, likens these creatures to voles living beneath the snow. A yellow rail conceals itself in a canopy of sedges, the bird's narrow body, strong toes, and rounded, agile wings enabling it to maneuver easily in the dense vegetation. Its unique manner of placing one foot directly in front of the other leaves a straight line of tracks, sometimes the only sign that a yellow rail is nearby. During breeding season, the yellow rail rarely flies; when it does, its short, weak flight lasts for mere seconds before it buries itself into another patch of tall, slender sedges.

Somehow, though, the yellow rail manages to fly south to the coastal marshes of North Carolina and Texas for the winter. During its migration, it stops to feed in wet cornfields; a farmer plowing his Illinois field one spring discovered two male yellow rails that had apparently stopped on their way from Texas back to Michigan. Birders intent on finding the bird outside of its breeding season walk through miles of wet fields hoping to stumble on the yellow treasure. But if they really want a good chance of seeing the yellow rail, they must go to Seney.

Part of the Great Manistique Swamp, Seney consists of a fairly level sand plain of sedge marshes, black spruce bog, seasonally flooded meadows, and higher grounds supporting jack, red, and white pines. Marshlands, black spruces, and white pines dominated the area before settlement. After the late 1800s, when loggers sold the land to farmers who could not get crops to grow, Seney reverted to the state of Michigan for taxes. In the 1930s, the Civilian Conservation Corps rebuilt the area as a wildlife refuge, constructing one hundred miles of dikes. Some seven thousand acres of water are impounded on the refuge. Land managers regulate water on twenty-one of twenty-six pools to provide habitat for rare or unique bird species such as bald eagles, sandhill cranes, common loons, black terns, and trumpeter swans. Nearly extirpated from the state, the trumpeter swan once again breeds here because of human reintroduction.

Arriving in early May each year, the yellow rail nests at Seney because of the fine mat of sedges, specifically *Carex lasiocarpa,* that grow here. "This natural habitat has always been at Seney," says Urbanek. "Yellow rails may well have been nesting here for centuries." It seems remarkable that considering all the disturbances the Seney refuge has undergone, the yellow rail would continue coming here. The species also breeds in a few remote, wet areas in Hiawatha National Forest and Houghton Lake in the Lower Peninsula, as well as in Wisconsin, the MacGregor Marsh in Minnesota, and across the northern provinces of Canada and eastern Asia. A small isolated population has also bred in Mexico.

Marsh Creek Pool, in the heart of the refuge, seems to be the hot spot for yellow rails at Seney. Here Urbanek and other researchers have banded and fit rails with radiotelemetric devices. Each night in late spring, at about 11 P.M., they go out to band the rails. "You find a rail, clap rocks together, and the male comes right to you," says Urbanek. "The male hears that sound and he comes right out. You grab it with a net and band it. After you band him and place him down, if you make the sound, he'll peck right at your hand. They think the sound is another male calling in their territory. They move in on the call to drive the male out."

"It takes lots of effort to see a yellow rail," says Urbanek. "The general John Q. Public has to go out with a guide and only at night, because they usually only call at night. But once you can find them, they seem very tame." Often when Urbanek takes a group out at midnight to find yellow rails, "they think we have a trained bird. One bird got so used to people that he used light from our flashlights to help him see while feeding. We watched him gulp down insect larvae." Humans, however, aren't prone to gulping down insect larvae, and Urbanek says you have two choices when going on a yellow rail tour: let the mosquitos bite you or let the mosquitos bite you. Even applying strong insect repellent doesn't always work, especially once out in the soggy sedges, where pockets of water harbor breeding mosquitos and the weather is so humid in summer that you imagine insect larvae hatch in midair.

While visitors slosh through the quicksand-like sedges just to see the yellow rail, Urbanek and Bookhout are out there to learn all they can about the bird, which is threatened in Michigan, so that it will continue to nest at Seney. They begin imitating the bird's call after quietly approaching to within thirty-five yards of a calling male. One or two other persons equipped with hand nets stand motionless, their nets poised. One of them shines a flashlight in an area in front of the person imitating the call. Someone taps together two objects, typically rocks, held six to eight inches above the ground. Stenzel also found that tapping a closed pocketknife against the femur bone from a young deer provided a resonant tone that attracted the birds. The male yellow rail usually responds by approaching the intruder, commonly walking or flying up to the person tapping the knife and bone or two rocks together, and then one of the researchers can capture the bird by hand or in a net. The bander grasps the bird's legs between his or her fingers, holding the wings shut so the bird can't fly.

Sometimes, when a bird is flushed, the banders must pursue it, stumbling in hip-high boots through the peaty muck. The experienced Urbanek insists "you can catch the yellow rails over and over and they still don't learn to be wary of banders," yet two young interns not quite adept at grabbing the rail found themselves uncomfortably knee-deep in sedges and slime with no bird in hand—and no luck the rest of the night. You have to wonder if the yellow rails play games with young banders at 1 A.M. Perhaps the mud-sinking experience is a required initiation rite for neophyte rail banders.

Banding and studying the yellow rails have yielded some surprising results. For instance, research at Seney shows that despite the nonstop nighttime calling of rails, the species is far from being nocturnal. Yellow rails form pairs and feed during the day, making them a diurnal species. But during the day, the birds melt into the vegetation and are impossible to catch.

The female builds her five-inch-wide nest of thin grasses in this vegetation, concealing it with some dead plants on top. She then lays five to ten oval, buff-colored eggs. In other rail species, both sexes share in incubation. But the polygynous male yellow rail expends his energies mating with several different females. So the female incubates alone, sitting on her nest nearly all day and all night long, leaving only briefly to dine on snails, aquatic insects, and seeds.

In eighteen days, the young hatch as black, fuzzy balls with bright pink bills, waiting for their mother to bring them mealworms she has softened by dunking in water and biting with her bill. Two days after they hatch, the chicks follow their mother on short feeding journeys.

Within three weeks, the chicks eat on their own, then leave with the other rails to migrate south.

Will the chicks or their parents return to the same place to breed next year? The Seney researchers have learned that though other avian species generally return to their same breeding sites year after year, the yellow rail does not. "In fact, we find that they are not even faithful to the area," says Urbanek. Out of two hundred rails Urbanek banded in the past seventeen years, only two returned to sites previously used. How a new bird finds Seney each year is another mystery locked somewhere in the bird's instinctual consciousness. In 1987, Urbanek took birds and mixed them up and moved them up to fourteen miles away from their territory. "I wanted to see if they would fly back to the same place," he says. "Any other bird would have flown right back, but not the yellow rails. There was no pattern. Some flew back. Some remained in the new spot, and others disappeared."

The nighttime rail banders have also found that proper habitat is essential to the yellow rail's breeding survival. Until recently, Seney refuge land managers maintained yellow rail habitat with controlled fires. Marshes had been naturally sustained by fire before settlers arrived. Fire kept trees from encroaching on marshland. Wildlife refuge workers have burned one thousand acres here in recent springs. "The conditions have to be right to burn, and it's very expensive," says Urbanek. "You can't have high winds and there can't be too much humidity." The burning kills the tag alder shrub, a successive marsh species that crowds out the sedge mats upon which yellow rails nest. Research by a graduate student suggested the rails prefer areas that were burned several years previously, so burning every year doesn't make sense, at least when it comes to managing for rails. Proper water levels are also necessary for the sedges to survive. A full-time fire ecologist once managed the burns for rails and other species, but has since left and has not been replaced.

Still, the data Urbanek and others have gathered on yellow rails supports the inclusion of this species on Michigan's threatened list. "The rail won't be delisted because its habitat requirement is so specific, but it won't become endangered, unless there's a sudden population decline," says Urbanek.

Yellow rail populations at Seney declined between 1995 and 1998. Urbanek says that could be due to the unusually cold winters, when snow remained on the ground well into May. "In 1994, we had eighty nesting pairs of yellow rails at Seney," he says. In spring 1998, only eight pairs nested. But knowing what is happening is difficult, since yellow rails don't return to their natal homes in spring. This species may have just found another place to breed in the years following the harsh winters.

Only time will determine the fate of the yellow rail at Seney National Wildlife Refuge, and to determine how well this species is faring, people like Urbanek will continue to go out in hip waders each spring to band an elusive bird that goes *Kick Kick Kickee Kick* in the night.

Spruce Grouse

April Dancers

DRIZZLE AND COLD GREET THE DAWN on a late April day in a field of short grasses, reindeer moss, and bloodred-tipped lichen. On a fifteen-foot-high, thirty-foot-wide ridge near Raco, Michigan, in the eastern UP, the male dancers appear. Dressed to the nines, they sport bright yellow eye combs, inflatable lavender neck sacs, and stiff tail feathers so white they can be seen a half mile away. From that distance, these northland creatures appear to be engaging in a wanton square dance.

Do si do, a caller might say as the male sharp-tailed grouse run around each other, never touching. Join hands, the caller might say, as the males lunge toward another, cooing. Kick your feet. Swing your partner. The males stomp, their feet blur.

Meanwhile, in a jack pine forest where snow still covers shaded areas and tamaracks thrive in moist bogs, the male spruce grouse struts in a forest clearing. Chest feathers puffed, he claps his wings, stomps his feet, and fans his erect tail feathers. His fiery scarlet eye combs shimmer like bright flares in the dimly lit forest.

Less beautifully colored but more vocal, a female penetrates the forest with her wheezing bellow to encourage the courtship. Minutes later, she sits ensconced on a jack pine, munching quietly on needles.

THUMP. THUMP. THUMP. THUMP. THUMP. THUMP. THUMP. THUMP. Thumpthumpthumpthumpthumpthump.

The ruffed grouse's wings beat slowly, then fast, faster, faster on a moss-covered log at the forest's edge. The sound echoes in the dark hours before dawn. A female investigates to decide if she will attend the dance.

The male is eighteen inches tall and sports a rufous tail conspicuously banded with black at the tip. He raises the black ruff around his neck. *Quit Quit Cluck Cluck Coo*, he says to her. Would you like to dance?

As the late April days lengthen, male sharp-tailed, spruce, and ruffed grouse begin to dance, like young men come after a hard day's work to swing their partners in an open-door barn lit by the moon. The grouse display their colors, ruffle their feathers, and fan large, wide tails to seek their dancing partners and to ward off the other males.

When the grouse emerge, Rick Baetsen's annual rite of spring begins. Baetsen travels in his pickup truck, sometimes with wife, children, and dog, to spend cold days and even colder nights in remote areas to study the grouse of Michigan's Upper Peninsula. Baetsen, a tall man possessing a wisdom of the wild that can be gained only from his forty-five years of experience living here, has sought sharp-tailed grouse in the grasslands, spruce grouse in the boreal forests, and ruffed grouse in hardwood forest edges. He has entered their secret lives, like a child exploring his own magical garden. He has observed courtship behavior, recorded data, and espoused his belief that their world needs saving.

A former U.S. Fish and Wildlife Service employee forced to leave his job after developing health problems, Baetsen maintains the enthusiasm of a child. He speaks in a rapid pace about the successes and failures of the grouse that live in the UP. He is, in fact, the savior of the sharp-tailed grouse, a bird he once thought would never display its thrilling courtship ritual for his grandchildren, just as he thought he might never fully recover from his illness. At least for now, the grouse are saved, and Baetsen's health is fairly stable.

An award-winning wildlife photographer, biologist, researcher, lover of the UP forests and all the creatures that dwell within them, a family man, and a stubborn wildlife advocate, Baetsen began his life in Akron, Michigan, a town with fewer than five hundred people. This Lower Peninsula community did not resemble the Upper Peninsula Baetsen has come to consider his second home. "Where I grew up, it was so flat," he says. "It was all farm fields. There were no big woods." His parents took him to the big woods. They had a cabin where they hiked and went snowshoeing. The cabin had no electricity and no running water, so Baetsen learned to live simply, what he calls "toughing it out."

His father taught high school shop, his mother was a homemaker. They taught Baetsen to do what he loved, and they taught him to love the outdoors just by bringing him there and letting him explore. They believed in pursuing education, not for glory, but for the thrill of learning. No wonder that Baetsen's library is filled with books he will never have the time to read, books on bees and butterflies, trees and sparrows, geology and lakes.

Even the quiet, farming community of Akron, with one school for sixty-four pupils, offered something to quench Baetsen's thirst for outdoor learning. He joined the Youth Conservation Club, built wood-duck boxes, and took an advanced biology class. He also went exploring on his own. One spring day when camping with his parents, Baetsen recalls, "I came upon this bird strutting—a large chicken-like bird with a beautiful black band on its tail." This was Baetsen's first look at a ruffed grouse, a bird many American children today only see on the Discovery Channel.

Was it this experience that thrust Baetsen into his life's work? He's not sure, but he does know that "when you experience nature up close and learn about behavior, you remember it. You remember seeing this living creature moving around in its own habitat, and feeling you're part of its world."

Baetsen could have attended Michigan State University, but instead he opted for the much smaller Lake Superior State College in Sault Ste. Marie, which he likened to a large high school in size. "I wanted to go up north. I wanted to go to the UP," he says. There he studied biology and spent days walking along the hemlock-lined Tahquamenon River, the barren, sandy edge of Lake Superior, and the deep woods of Hiawatha National Forest. "The big forests, the big lakes were there," he says. "And I was in the middle of it."

Baetsen also met his future wife, Bonnie Heuvelhorst, in a botany class at college. She, too, was studying biology, as well as medical technology. A Michigan native, Bonnie developed her appreciation for the natural world as a high school student living in Newberry, in the UP.

Her family camped and took vacations to see the country. While in college, Rick and Bonnie took a class that required a botany field trip in April of 1974 to the Smoky Mountains. "Most of the girls on the trip stayed in cabins in town, but Bonnie and one other girl stayed in tents with the rest of us guys who were camping outside of town," he says.

After he graduated in 1975, Baetsen worked for the Michigan Department of Natural Resources and the U.S. Forest Service as a fish biologist near the land he loved. In 1978, Bonnie and Rick married. They spent their honeymoon not in the Bahamas or on a cruise, but at the flat Raco Plains in Chippewa County, about forty-four miles southeast of Whitefish Point. One morning at 5 A.M., they hiked in the dark, squinting at the hint of light in the east. A distant cooing beckoned them into scratchy pine plantations and then out into an open field laden with blueberry bushes and lichens. With the rising sun at their backs, they saw, through binoculars, the sharp-tails dancing like spirits around a ring. The fifteen-to-twenty-inch-tall birds with short, pointed tails, arched their wings, spun, and performed on a raised furrow, the birds' booming grounds. "They seemed to magically disappear and then reappear as they moved from one side over to the other," says Baetsen.

The newly married couple crawled on their stomachs on the cold, damp ground to get to within fifty yards of the birds. The grouse froze, then thunderously burst into the air, a tactic grassland birds use to confuse predators. The couple examined the booming grounds, where the spring dances take place, noticing bowl-like depressions where the grouse had danced. They also saw feathers that had been pulled out during confrontations between males. They then left quickly so the sharp-tails would return.

Knowing that disturbing wildlife during courtship could affect reproduction success, Rick began using blinds built with two-by-two-inch wooden stakes and a burlap support to watch the birds. From the blind on cold April and May days, he observed the intricate courtship and territorial defense of the sharp-tail, the grouse most inextricably linked to the UP's ecological history. This species' population has risen, then fallen, due to human manipulation of the ecosystem and natural ecological succession.

Before settlement, the UP consisted mostly of forest and wetlands such as marshes and bogs. These ecosystems did not provide much habitat for the sharp-tail, which during courtship needs a minimum of one square mile of open land with short grasses for its booming grounds. Baetsen speculates that before humans came, isolated pockets of sharp-tails existed in the UP, and that before the arrival of settlers, local fires created openings in the land capable of supporting a small number of this species. No data are available to determine the status of sharp-tails before settlers came. But when they did, bringing their axes and plows, sharp-tails probably experienced a population rise. Settlers planted Juneberry, pin cherry, and aspen—good food sources for the sharp-tail. They logged extensive stands of white, red, and jack pines, creating forest openings. Intense fires, either accidental or a result of lightning strikes, burned the limited nutrients that might have decayed and been returned to the soil to support more trees. These tracts of once-forested land became open, short-grass prairies, and the sharp-tail population began to grow.

The first written record of sharp-tails in the Upper Peninsula is from August 31, 1890, when a lighthouse keeper on what is now Isle Royale National Park discovered them while picking raspberries. Young sharp-tails were seen again on the island in 1912. By 1920, the species inhabited the western part of the UP and was slowly moving eastward. In 1951, sharp-tailed grouse were found in all fifteen counties in the Upper Peninsula. Their numbers totaled between three thousand and five thousand birds.

The greater prairie-chicken, a species that also needs large tracts of grassland for breeding, also expanded its range to the UP in the early 1900s, reaching a population peak in the 1930s. But by 1956, only a few if any colonies were found in that region of Michigan. Today, the prairie-chicken is gone from Michigan. The last prairie-chicken Baetsen saw in the Wolverine State was near Marion in April 1979. None have been found since 1981.

But the sharp-tailed grouse hangs on in northern Michigan, as well as in Alaska, Canada, and some of the northwestern states, but no longer in its former territories in Oregon, Nevada, and New Mexico. Perhaps the sharp-tailed grouse is able to remain in the UP because it requires smaller territories than the prairie-chicken. After the loggers left, forests regenerated, reducing the size of the UP's grasslands. Sharp-tails moved into areas that could no longer support prairie-chickens. Jack pines thrived in this changing ecosystem, able to adapt to sandy soils, which are not fertile enough for deciduous trees. So the spread of woody growth was at first retarded, allowing the sharp-tails some areas in which to court and reproduce.

Ideal sharp-tail habitat includes 40 acres of open area for dancing surrounded by 320 acres of 20 percent woody cover scattered with tree clumps, small brushy areas, and open grasslands. Many such areas existed during the pioneer days.

Over the years, Baetsen has attempted to locate as many sharp-tail leks, or dancing grounds, as he could find in the east and central parts of the UP, from Munising near Pictured Rocks National Lakeshore east to Drummond Island. Baetsen discovered that each male has its own territory within a lek. The males define their territories with imaginary lines, like those drawn by siblings in shared bedrooms. The dominant grouse holds center stage. Secondary grouse territories flank either side of the center, with tertiary territories farther away. Face-offs occur at the territory boundaries and the dancing often starts simultaneously, as if on cue.

The males inflate and deflate their lavender neck sacs, creating the telltale cooing sound. They erect their white tail feathers and rattle them back and forth, with wings arched and extended. They stomp their feet, moving in a loose circle. If one male gets too close to another's boundary, the two birds might fight with the beak or feet and sometimes in the air. Baetsen has seen a dominant bird on one lek displaced to a satellite position after getting injured in a skirmish.

To witness this remarkable display, humans must arrive on the lek before even a hint of daylight. One cold, windy, misty day at 4 A.M., I joined Baetsen and some birders at a lek site. I wore several layers for warmth, including two pairs of long underwear, three pairs of socks, and heavy-duty winter boots. Three or four of us crunched in several different blinds in the dark, packed in tighter than four people in a one-person tent. Even in these close quarters, my feet were numb with cold. We had to be still, quiet, and patient. Time passed slowly. When a vesper sparrow began singing from a group of shrub trees bordering the flat grassland, my pulse leapt. But only the sparrow sang. As light emerged, we still saw no sharp-tails. Fidgeting to reduce the pain in my legs and the impatience in my soul, I shivered. More time passed.

Then, a loud flutter echoed past the blind. What was that? Another loud flutter. Wings. Sharp-tail wings. Still, we had to be quiet. Finally, when we heard a distant, resonant cooing, we edged our binoculars into a slit in the blind and saw them—the huge, burnt yellow eyebrows, the expanding red balloons at their necks where they produce the sounds, wings so outstretched you could see almost every individual feather, hovering to the ground. Tails straight up. It was then that I more fully appreciated Baetsen's passion for the sharp-tail. To understand, sometimes you must see.

After watching the males for a while, someone directed us to look for the less-conspicuous females, who lack the bright eye comb and wide tail feathers. An observer might not even notice the females amid the colorful display of the males, but they are there watching from the perimeter. Sometimes females walk right in the middle of things and have to dodge the males, who seem oblivious to their existence, even if they are not. We remained in the blinds until a good fifteen minutes after the males and females had left the lek to roost in aspens and young conifer stands.

The females arrive at the leks several weeks after the males have claimed their territories and started dancing. The females come into the lek later in the morning, after the males have been dancing for a while. They wander through the lek area, often pursued by a male and chased to the perimeter of the lek. Females choose the dominant males with which to mate. A male who puts on the best appearance or dances the best and is usually in the center of the lek mates with many females. The pairs typically mate in the center of the lek.

Once the females have mated, they leave the lek to choose their nest sites, preferably beneath a chokeberry, willow, or alder tree. The male's job done, he takes no part in raising young, leaving the female to incubate her ten to thirteen smooth, oval, buffy brown eggs. Within three weeks, the young hatch. The chicks are tempting treats for raptors and other predators, so the female often moves her young to woodsier cover for protection. The sharp-tail young eat mainly insects, including grasshoppers, small bugs, and caterpillars. They also dine on strawberries as well as the leaves, buds, and flowers of deciduous and coniferous trees.

From the late 1970s through the 1980s, Baetson watched as sharp-tail populations rose from a few to ten, eleven, or more males on one lek and then dwindled until the birds disappeared. A lek in Otsego County in the northern part of Lower Michigan once supported nineteen dancing males, but by the mid-1980s, they were all gone. Baetsen said that in 1977, the Michigan Natural Resources Commission placed a five-year moratorium on sharp-tailed grouse hunting, then lifted it in 1978, saying the population had rebounded sufficiently to open the season. Bemoaning the continual decline of the sharp-tail population, Baetsen helped form the Michigan Sharp-tailed Grouse Association in 1989 to survey habitat and populations of the species. The members, aside from Baetsen, are mostly hunters. Baetsen instead hunts with his camera, doing photography work as well as freelance biological research for diverse private and governmental institutions such as the Michigan Nature Association and the U.S. Forest Service.

Just as the sharp-tail's numbers declined, Baetsen became afflicted with a chronic illness called Crohn's disease. The illness has greatly altered his lifestyle and influenced his way of thinking. "I now better know what is important in life and how to spend my time," he says.

One of the ways he decided to spend his time was working to save his beloved sharp-tailed grouse. "Sharp-tail numbers were declining so rapidly that the species may have been extirpated from the Upper Peninsula, indeed all of Michigan, by the early part of the twenty-first century," he says. A combination of mild winters, habitat change and loss, as well as fewer dollars available for habitat management contributed to the species' decline. Reforestation, such as the planting of red pines, diminishes the open areas that sharp-tails need. Red pines provide little sustenance for sharp-tails; they offer no nutrition for many of the Upper Peninsula's species.

Sharp-tails prefer the heavy snows that typically dominate northern Michigan's winters. To hide from predators and protect themselves from the cold, sharp-tails roost beneath the snow when it is deep enough, typically near sparse jack pine cover. They leave during the day to feed on crops or aspen buds. But with little snow for protection in the late 1980s and early 1990s, sharp-tails became more susceptible to predation. Meanwhile, species that prey on ruffed and sharp-tailed grouse, such as snowy owls, coyotes, raccoons, skunks, and red foxes, were experiencing population increases.

Baetsen wrote letter after letter, made phone call after phone call, and attended meeting after meeting to convince area officials to help save the sharp-tails. One person who listened, although he did not agree with everything Baetson proposed, was John Urbain, forest game-bird specialist for the Michigan Department of Natural Resources. "Rick Baetsen is certainly dedicated to protecting the sharp-tailed grouse in the UP," says Urbain, who agrees that sharp-tail numbers have declined. "The surveys conducted since the early 1990s show that the number of dancing grouse on leks has declined 45 to 65 percent in Michigan," he says. "Similar declines have been shown in other parts of the sharp-tail range from Wisconsin and Minnesota." Baetsen puts it more simply, more harshly. "In 1996, only one hundred dancing males were left in the UP."

And yet, considering that the UP once barely supported sharp-tails, would it not be more prudent to let nature be the final judge? The Michigan DNR has tried in the past to maintain large clearings in the UP to help the sharp-tailed grouse, but keeping the forest at bay is not easy, says Urbain. "It is expensive," he says, "and the forest is winning."

Perhaps that is the way it should be. But Baetsen argues that humans have reshaped the environment and now must work to maintain it for the sustenance of species such as the sharp-tail. And what of the non-native species such as rainbow trout, brown trout, and ring-necked pheasants that are being managed in the state for anglers and hunters? Baetsen poses this question to anyone who tells him sharp-tailed grouse don't belong on the UP. "I've certainly been a voice, perhaps one some people haven't wanted to hear, but a voice."

It took some time, but in 1994, Baetsen convinced officials to agree to some restrictions on the sharp-tail hunting season in the UP, and in

1996, the state put a moratorium on sharp-tailed grouse hunting state-wide. Urbain says a new Lake Superior State Forest plan will include the management of large-opening complexes in the UP to support a wide variety of grassland species, whose numbers are declining nationwide due to loss of habitat. "Certainly the sharp-tail should warrant consideration," he says, adding that Baetsen's involvement with the planning process "is critical."

The U.S. Forest Service periodically burns 1,000 acres to maintain grassland areas, and also planted 150 acres with grasses, and created 300 acres of openings for sharp-tails in Hiawatha National Forest. The U.S. Fish and Wildlife Service at Seney National Wildlife Refuge has established nearly 1,500 acres to be managed for grassland species. "Sharp-tail numbers responded to this increased habitat," says Baetsen, "and counts of males on dancing grounds there increased from five in 1991 to twenty-seven in 1995. On leks I surveyed in 1998, the birds were up 30 percent at Seney. I found twenty-nine birds just on one dancing ground."

Baetsen remains vigilant. He continues to argue with Urbain over whether the sharp-tail species is native to the UP. John Ries, president of the Michigan Sharp-tailed Grouse Association, has gained support of some of the chapters of the Michigan United Conservation Club, which has one hundred thousand members who are mostly hunters and anglers. Baetsen and these members might seem strange bedfellows, but hunters, for the most part, support the conservation of species such as the sharp-tailed grouse. Their fees help pay for habitat enhancement. "And habitat is the key to survival of all species," Baetsen says.

Baetsen continues to search for sharp-tailed grouse in the UP, firmly convinced a place exists for the species there. He contacts hunters, conservation biologists, reporters—anyone who can influence what will happen to the sharp-tailed grouse in the UP.

He is not, however, content to just watch the sharp-tailed grouse. An eclectic naturalist who gets equally excited about sharp-tails, fritillary butterflies, and other wild creatures, Baetsen has traveled with his wife and three children—Amy, the youngest, Ryan, and Justin, the eldest—to observe nesting Pacific loons and willow ptarmigans in the Yukon Territory, to create videos of the butterflies of Michigan, and to camp in the Rocky Mountains. "As a family we see many more things than we would by ourselves," says Baetsen. "Bonnie points out flowers that I might have just overstepped while watching or listening to a bird in the distance, and Ryan spots a ptarmigan near the road edge, or a moose with a calf that was right on the road edge in a park in Alberta, that I had just driven by. Bonnie and I want to expose our children to all the neat things we know of and can find, not to overwhelm them with our interests, but to encourage them to pursue what they find interesting, as others have done for us."

Baetsen takes his children out at night to survey the nocturnal northern saw-whet owl, which sings a melancholy, one-pitched song during mating season. One night, Baetsen and several of his biologist friends working on saw-whet owl surveys encountered a rare natural event. While the northern lights hung with a full moon in the sky, snowshoe hares performed a magical dance that Baetsen had only read about. The snowshoe hare, active at night, has long, heavily furred toes covered with stiff, thick hairs, enabling it to walk or even bound over fluffy snow without sinking. Typically a solitary creature, the hare becomes more social in spring during courtship and territorial defense. It is in spring that hares sometimes "dance" beneath a full moon.

"We found ourselves moving closer and closer toward the edge of the field to watch the hares dance on three feet of snow," says Baetsen. "Several hares, maybe more, were running around on all four feet and then sometimes jumping up on their hind feet and hopping. They, on occasion, would approach each other or at least pass by each other during their movements. With only the moonlight, it was ghostlike. All we saw were quick movements of grayish white animals. The hares continued this activity, even though I was right on the fringe of where they were dancing. . . . I remember the hairs raising on my neck as I watched them. It was not so much a spiritual experience, as it was a natural experience," the kind that proves everything is possible and some things cannot be explained. Little is known about why the hares dance under a full moon, and few people have witnessed the event.

"It could be that all the animals that I saw were males putting on some sort of courtship display. But I like to believe in the myth that the hares were actually dancing beneath a full moon and the most beautiful display of northern lights I had ever seen."

Baetsen cannot explain why fully, but he does know that he wants humans to enjoy all these experiences—the rabbits dancing, the sharp-tailed grouse dancing, and the spruce grouse performing their unique courtship ritual within the boreal forest.

While somewhat abundant in suitable habitat in the Upper Peninsula, the spruce grouse is extremely rare in the Lower Peninsula. Baetsen began searching for spruce grouse in 1981 near Whitefish Bay when he learned of a bird that was supposedly so tame it would stand right in the middle of the road. Legend says a spruce grouse will sit quietly on branches, even allowing humans to beat it with a stick. From this unseemly myth, the spruce grouse was nicknamed "fool hen." Yet finding the male spruce grouse, with scarlet eye combs, white-and-black chest feathers, and white and buffy tail tips, was nearly impossible. And trying to locate the drabber female, with mottled gray, brown, and black camouflage hues, was deemed downright futile. Not one to eschew challenges, Baetsen began looking for the elusive spruce grouse. He drove miles of winding, narrow forest roads, for hours, for days, without finding a single spruce grouse. The species became his nemesis. It was a magical bird, no doubt. He speculated that just as with the unicorn, people told tales about this bird, but no one had actually ever seen one. It was difficult to decide if he or the bird were the bigger fool.

Baetsen's search lead him to the book *Spruce Grouse: Fool Hen of the Yellow Dog Plains,* by William Robinson. The scientist had conducted a major study of the biology of these birds and their habitat in the Yellow Dog Plains, a glacial plain forested by jack pine and spruce covering twenty-five square miles in Marquette County in the north-central UP. Robinson's book suggested that to find a spruce grouse, a birder should search for droppings and dust bowls, depressions in the earth where grouse splash in the dust to get rid of mites. Baetsen began looking for signs, but even when he found droppings or bowls, he could not find the bird.

Then, one hot August day while driving a back road through a coniferous forest, Baetsen saw dark figures in the middle of the road. He stopped, then gasped. A male spruce grouse with a female and three young birds were there right in front of him. Baetsen had been wandering in thick woods searching pine thicket after pine thicket for the birds, and here was an entire family, out in the road. The female and young slipped into the woods. The male hopped on a jack pine branch and began munching on needles, a major part of the species' diet.

As in the case of many birding experiences, as soon as Baetsen saw his first spruce grouse, he found it easier to locate more. One male was so tame that Baetsen was able to touch its feet and feel the feathers down to the toenails.

One late April day in 1991, Baetsen, a group of birders, and I caravanned several miles from Whitefish Point down a back road bordered by a wet bog of jack pine, tamarack, and black spruce. We walked through a pine forest searching for the male spruce grouse that Baetsen had seen there earlier. Boreal chickadees called their drawling *chick-a-day-day-day,* and the elusive gray jay quickly appeared and then disappeared back into the pines. We wore layered clothing, but the chill we had felt earlier subsided when we ventured into the dense forest, making some of us even too warm for comfort. A dewy, evergreen scent pleasantly filled each breath, but after a half hour of walking without any luck, pleasure was replaced with fatigue.

To encourage the spruce grouse to emerge, Baetsen played a tape of the female's vocalization. She seeks her mate with a bellowing, whining call that only a male spruce grouse would love. She begins with a long series of clucks, loud at first, then decreasing in volume. Next comes three or four high-pitched whines. A male spruce grouse, unable to resist the taped invitation, appeared from underneath a pine. His scarlet eye combs were so enlarged they almost touched. He puffed out his black-and-white chest feathers, dropped his wings, and raised his tail feathers, showing off a distinctive yellow band. He strutted on the ground in a flat open area within the woods and hopped on lower branches of trees, interjecting his display with wing claps and foot stomps. To human eyes, the male appeared totally entranced with the object of his amours.

Once she gets her man, the female avoids the male and searches for a nest site, where she arranges grasses and leaves beneath low evergreen branches or at the base of a small conifer. There she lays her five to ten cinnamon-colored eggs, boldly marked with rich brown spots. The female incubates alone, with the eggs hatching in about three weeks. A week after hatching, the young begin fluttering about on the ground, learning how to find pine needles for nourishment.

In his research, Baetsen plays tapes to attract the spruce grouse as a necessary step to accurately document their presence, but he prefers not to use that method when taking groups out to find the bird. Minimizing disturbance during nesting season is important. Instead, he leads groups on a search for droppings. Walking between jack pines and spruces and enjoying the April freshness during another foray into spruce grouse territory, a group of birders and I searched for droppings about one-inch long and one-fourth-inch wide. The greener they are, the fresher they are, and their earthy odor is not at all objectionable to humans. The droppings contain the pine needles the grouse eat. Spruce grouse cannot digest the needles, but glean life-sustaining nutrients from them. They subsist almost entirely on jack pine needles in the winter, somehow knowing which trees contain the highest protein and ash content, what scientists refer to as superior trees. In spring, spruce grouse also eat trailing arbutus flowers, blueberry buds, and bunchberry leaves.

We located several areas with brownish droppings, then split, agreeing to raise a hand if a grouse was found. When the group reconvened, one woman was not there. She had stumbled on a log and then looked down to see a female spruce grouse sitting and looking back at her. The woman ran to tell the group, and when she led us to the spot, the female grouse was still there, resting on the log as we watched from a distance. The grouse moved a bit, ruffled her feathers, and flew from sight. We examined the fine, fresh droppings at the log, then looked up to see the female sitting on a pine tree nibbling on needles, like a magic leprechaun laughing at humans from a perch in a tree.

Baetsen has studied spruce grouse territories and learned some new information about this secretive and little-studied bird. He surveyed two areas on the Raco Plains, twenty-five miles southwest of Sault Ste. Marie in Hiawatha National Forest, between April 28 and May 30, 1993. One area consisted of mature forest stands of jack pine with some younger stands of jack and red pines. The other area, near a creek, contained mature jack pines, red pine, recent forest clear-cuts, jack and red pine regeneration, and swamp conifers such as cedar and black spruce.

Jack pines have curved, one-inch-long, twisted needles and small, tight, brown cones. The trees look unkempt and bedraggled. Red pines have six-inch-long, soft needles and shiny, oblong cones. These stately trees can grow to seventy-five feet and commonly lack lower branches when they get that tall. Cedars have flat, thin, scaly needles that look like tentacles extending from the trunk. Black spruces are the true cold-climate conifers, unable to grow south of the Virginia mountains. They have bluish green, half-inch-long needles and grow to forty feet tall. If the spruce grouse is a magical creature, the forest in which it lives is magical, too.

Among these strikingly handsome trees, Baetsen and Tom Kurtz of the U.S. Forest Service randomly selected four quarter sections within a four-square-mile area to study. Then Baetsen ran north-south transect survey lines in which they broadcast taped recordings of the female spruce grouse's territorial call. He listened in between the recordings for responding calls and the thundering sound of males performing aerial drumming flights. Male spruce grouse declare their territories by ascending into the air on rapidly beating wings. Then they descend quietly to the ground or a tree branch. Baetsen observed and documented the presence of spruce grouse in the mature forest stands, as he had expected. He also found that although spruce grouse have been known to frequent the boreal forests, especially those bordering bogs and marshes with black spruce and tamarack, they will also court, display, and nest in drier areas. In fact, Baetsen found twice as many spruce grouse in the drier jack pine stands than in wetter areas he surveyed.

Much of the best spruce grouse habitat exists on state and federal land, which affords the species some protection. Hunting of this species is prohibited in Michigan, although Minnesota and some other states allow it. In 1990, the Michigan Nature Association created a sanctuary for the spruce grouse in a two-hundred-acre parcel in Schoolcraft County near Seney National Wildlife Refuge. Baetsen had discovered four displaying males in the area. Baetson has since located three male and two female grouse on the sanctuary property, and he conducts spruce grouse tours there each spring.

Spruce grouse numbers are declining at the Yellow Dog Plains area in Marquette County that Robinson studied in the 1960s. The Mead Corporation, the largest landowner in the UP, has purchased about 40 percent of potential spruce grouse habitat within the past ten years. Large clear-cuts in 1991 elicited angry phone calls from the public, according to the Spruce Grouse Society. A casual survey reported in the society's newsletter, *Fool-Hens Forever,* showed that "the number of spruce grouse on the Yellow Dog Plains is less than half of the 220 to 250 estimated in the 1960s." In December of 1991, Mead developed a new management plan that included leaving some uncut corridors connecting mature forest tracts to harbor some spruce grouse. Mead also planted new trees, albeit mostly red pines, which grow more quickly than other conifers. Red pine plantations do not sustain spruce grouse, providing neither good shelter nor sufficient nutrients. Mead now consults with scientists, including Robinson, about how to protect spruce grouse habitat while cutting forests to meet people's demands for paper.

Spruce grouse numbers declined during the harsh winters of 1997 and 1998, says Baetsen. A group of researchers continues to examine the habitat needs and population demographics of this tough-to-observe bird—protected from hunting but not from habitat change. And Baetsen remains ever vigilant, continuing his spruce grouse surveys to make sure this species does not go the way of the sharp-tail.

Much less rare than the spruce grouse, but equally as magical, is the ruffed grouse, one of Michigan's most popular game birds. This species fills an ecological niche that does not support spruce or sharp-tailed grouse. Ruffed grouse often choose young-growth forest in which to live. There they find the fruiting trees and shrubs they need for food and cover. Ruffed grouse live in thirty-eight of the United States and probably all of the Canadian provinces. These hearty, snow-loving, native birds can survive cold winters.

On an early morning, as you fish for trout in one of the UP's inland lakes or hike through the woods, a distant sound resembling that of a chain saw or lawn mower being started tells you the ruffed grouse has gone a-courting. Logs or occasionally mounds and boulders in the forest are the courtship settings of this sixteen-to-nineteen-inch-tall woodland drummer with a fan-shaped reddish to grayish tail tipped in black. The male may be at his log by 3 A.M. and full into drumming by 4 A.M. He may also drum all night long beneath a full moon or in the middle of the day beneath a scorching sun. Once on the log, the male fans his tail. He starts beating his wings slowly, increasing the speed until it sounds like a drumroll. He repeats the six-to-eight-second-long drumming every few minutes. The sound comes from air compression created by rapid wing movement. Once a female arrives, the male hops off the log and struts around his nuptial bed, fanning out his tail. He also raises the dark ruffs around his neck, so that he looks like a model in a dress with a black velvet collar.

When spring comes, the males defend territories of about six to ten acres with their drumming antics. Two females may live in this territory. Once the brief courtship ends, the mated female finds a hollow depression in leaf litter near trees or brush to lay her eight to fourteen buff-colored eggs. The female must camouflage her nest until the young hatch in five weeks.

As soon as they hatch, the young, though only the size of a small child's fist, are ready to leave the nest and search for food, mostly insects such as grasshoppers and crickets. Their mother may lead them as far as four miles from the nest to find food. Northern goshawks and great horned owls prey on the young.

The grouse's numbers rise and fall cyclically, apparently due to weather trends and food availability, and perhaps, more recently, to clear-cutting of forests and fire suppression. Natural periodic woodland fires help create the secondary niches ruffed grouse need. The Ruffed Grouse Society endorses forestry practices, such as selective cutting, that can maintain the bird's habitat. For now, the ruffed grouse population remains stable in the UP; but to be sure, Baetsen will start knocking on doors the moment he notices preventable problems with the bird's welfare.

Baetsen once discovered a ruffed grouse that he says was either considerably tame or extremely territorial. Near Indian Lake, close to the town of Manistique, lived a male ruffed grouse who had at least two females in his harem. For nearly two years, Baetsen experienced an unusual relationship with this particular bird, which responded to his voice. He visited and photographed the grouse, and named it Charlie. Whether in May, September, or December, when Baetsen approached Charlie, the bird tugged at his shirt or pecked at his hand. Since then, Baetsen has encountered two more seemingly tame ruffed grouse, one near Seney National Wildlife Refuge in the middle of the UP and one near Whitefish Point in the eastern UP. Baetsen spends time in spring and fall with his Seney grouse; many of his prize-winning photos of ruffed grouse are of a bird that allowed Baetsen and his son Ryan to sit in plain view on his log with him as he drummed.

I have not seen any of the ruffed grouse that Baetsen described to me. But I believe his stories. Consider the many years Rick Baetsen has spent his early mornings observing the unique dance of the courting sharp-tailed grouse in the UP. And consider that he has touched the feathered feet of his magical bird, the spruce grouse. Why then would anyone doubt that the ruffed grouse of Michigan's UP have formed a special kinship with the man who has been their friend and protector for a more than a quarter of a century?

Peregrine Falcon and Chicks

Life on the Edge

WEARING A HARD HAT and lugging a backpack full of D-shaped lock rings, ropes, seat harnesses, and binoculars, Joe Rogers descends a sandstone cliff overlooking Lake of the Clouds in the Porcupine Mountains. It's a one-hundred-foot vertical drop to the bottom of this cliff, one of many that punctuate the western UP. A V shape in the water below indicates a beaver gathering aquatic plants on which to dine. But Joe is way too high to actually see the beaver, even with binoculars.

"Let's go over this one more time," says Joe's wife, Barb. Her job is to let the rope down slowly as Joe descends. His gear can hold four thousand pounds. He weighs less than two hundred pounds. But, if he takes a fall, the force increases his weight one hundredfold.

"Your life is dependent on hanging on this gear," says Joe.

"We review every year so I do it right," says Barb, unable to resist adding, "This is the one time of year I can control him."

Joe Rogers has spent nearly one thousand nights with peregrine falcons in the UP. He has hiked through Isle Royale National Park, across Pictured Rocks National Lakeshore, and through hundreds of miles of mostly barren cliffs in the Porcupine Mountains and Ottawa National Forest. For the past decade, Rogers has left his home in the Lower Peninsula in April to drive five hundred miles to the UP. The five-foot, seven-inch-tall man with slightly graying, auburn brown hair and a matching beard travels fourteen hundred miles round-trip in his red Ford pickup, a makeshift camper in the back and several kayaks hoisted on top. Accompanying him are his mutt, Bonnie, and sometimes Barb, a tall, slender woman who often wears her long, dark, wavy hair in a neatly gathered ponytail.

"We have lived up here, sometimes, for 127 nights at a time," says Joe. We meaning Joe and his dog, Bonnie.

"You have to carry everything up there on your back," he says. "I've had four tents destroyed by bears and five others by thunderstorms." Replacing worn tents, climbing gear, spotting scopes, and other paraphernalia gets costly. Securing funds to continue his work is not always easy, especially now that the public, once enamored with the peregrine falcon, is now focused on other species. Rogers considers himself lucky if he breaks even. His wife is his biggest funder, he says. She teaches science to grade-school children so he can pursue his penchant for peregrines, and so they can both run their wildlife rehabilitation center in the Lower Peninsula and offer nature programs to inner-city schoolchildren in Detroit. When school is over, Barb comes north to help Joe.

On a June day so humid that sweat dampens your hair even while standing still, Joe ties several ropes to the side of a cliff on what little vegetation he can find at the top of the Escarpment Trail, overlooking Lake of the Clouds. The extra ropes are in case the ones he's holding break. With the cliff virtually barren except for patches of mosses, lichens, and an occasional stunted white pine, there's just not much to hang onto. Only the strong, whether human or plant, survive these harsh conditions, especially when late winter winds knock the breath out of even the heartiest mountain climber and when muggy, oppressive summer days make it difficult to inhale.

Joe Rogers begins the descent.

"I hope they have eggs," Barb says softly. She feeds Joe some rope, then stops. "Give me a little more," he calls. Bonnie barks at the sound of Joe's voice. Joe sounds hopeful, Barb thinks to herself. Minutes later, Joe reappears on top of the cliff. "No eggs," he says.

He is silent for a moment, then says, "I don't know what she's doing."

Joe has seen a courting pair of peregrine falcons here since early May. He has watched the couple pass sticks and scream and chase each other. He has observed them dive and yell at beavers and deer.

"But why hasn't she laid eggs?" says Joe. It's June 8. She should have laid eggs by now.

"It could be we've gotten the wrong hole. But if the nest was anyplace close, they'd be dive-bombing us," says Joe. Spring is late. The last of the snow didn't even melt until June. That means fewer bugs, fewer birds, and fewer prey for the peregrines.

Maybe the female has not yet laid her eggs. If so, the longer she waits, the less chance the young will survive, for the cold autumn winds will chase away their food, forcing them to migrate when they are not yet ready.

Historically, dozens of pairs of peregrine falcons bred in Michigan's UP near Pictured Rocks National Lakeshore, Isle Royale National Park, the Trap Hills in Ottawa National Forest, and the Porcupine Mountains. The species winters in Mexico, Central America, and South America, as well as some more northerly locations, including California and New Mexico. In spring, it migrates to breed as far north as Greenland, though some breed in South America. Peregrine falcons have bred on every continent except Antarctica.

The peregrines prefer open cliff areas, rocks, a ledge upon which to lay eggs, open areas for hunting songbirds and shorebirds, and, if possible, water beneath the cliffs. In the UP, Lake Superior and inland lakes beckon.

Joe Rogers has time to read about peregrine history while sitting at the bottom of a cliff for twelve hours in the steaming sun observing the bird's behavior. In the early 1800s, humans shot peregrine falcons in the UP. Peregrines were considered vermin, a nuisance.

Of course, some humans had a use for them. As early as 2000 B.C., Egyptians and the Chinese practiced falconry, the art of training raptors to hunt for a person. During medieval times, only certain classes of nobility were allowed to hunt with peregrines. Military officers used pigeons during wartime to send messages, and falcons were trained to nab the opposition's pigeons. "This went on for thousands of years," says Rogers. "During the first half of World War II, the U.S. Army maintained a pigeon corps and a falcon corps. The German army had the best falcon corps in the world."

A peregrine falcon gets its prey by first flying in the air to gather speed, then diving straight down—Rogers calls this the jay dive—curling one foot as if making a fist. The peregrine hits the prey with the curled foot to stun it. Then the falcon flies underneath the prey and grabs it in mid-air with its talons. Rogers calls this the accipiter ambush. When diving, a peregrine can reach 200 miles per hour, a necessity since it must be flying faster than its prey in order to catch it.

This remarkable feat makes a peregrine falcon seem indomitable. It is not. The laws of nature dictate that each species possesses adaptations so it can eat and reproduce, but each species also encounters obstacles so that it will not totally dominate. A peregrine's obstacle is that it can only catch its prey in the open. A peregrine can't fly fast through trees like the Cooper's hawk or sharp-shinned hawk. The peregrine may be known as the ultimate predator, but its special hunting techniques also leave it vulnerable to environmental changes.

"Peregrines are mentally tough," says Brian Kenner, resource management specialist for Pictured Rocks National Lakeshore. "Evolution has made them that way. But nothing prepared them for chemicals." Habitat loss as well as hunting and egg collecting also contributed to the decline of peregrines, but not nearly to the extent that pesticides, including DDT had, says Mary Hennen, a Chicago Academy of Sciences biologist who directs the Chicago Peregrine Release and Restoration Project.

In the early twentieth century, an estimated three hundred to four hundred peregrines nested east of the Rocky Mountains; by the 1960s, they were all gone. Similar scenarios were playing out in many parts of the world. Scientists linked the population crashes to the use of DDT, a pesticide designed to increase crop production. DDT was touted as the chemical of the future, the way to feed the world, but limited human knowledge at the time made it difficult to know the effects it would have on wildlife and people. When biologists began recording a major decline in the breeding success of the peregrine falcon, the bald eagle, and other birds at the top of the food chain, the curse of DDT was slowly unveiled.

"DDT is a neurotoxin. It makes the male peregrines clumsier. They are unable to hunt well," says Rogers. How DDT affects female peregrines is more complicated. When a female ingests DDT-contaminated prey, she absorbs it in her system, which interrupts the flow of calcium to the eggs. The female produces eggs with shells so weak they break upon the slightest shock.

In the 1970s, biologists worldwide met to discuss the decline and what could be done to reverse it. Banning the use of DDT in the United

States, where much of it was produced, became crucial to the falcon's recovery; however, that alone would not solve the problem. Scientists also faced the challenge of assisting those peregrines that were still laying thin eggs, as well as returning the falcon to areas where it used to breed.

Where peregrines were still nesting, the weight of the male and female incubating the too-thin eggs crushed them. Biologists scaled the cliffs, carefully removed the eggs, and left dummy eggs so the parents would continue incubating. Researchers placed the eggs in an incubator in which the temperature and lighting conditions simulated that of the nest, maintaining the eggs at the same temperature as a female would sitting on them. After the eggs hatched, biologists fed the young until they were a few weeks old, then returned them to the nest. Biologists fed the young with surrogate peregrine puppets that slip over the arms. The young saw only the puppets, and not the humans, so they did not imprint on the humans. If a peregrine learned a human was its source of food, it might not be able to survive when placed back in the wild.

"Peregrines were also captive-bred and the eggs taken from the parents," says Hennen, who has helped release these birds at the top of Chicago skyscrapers. "By removing the eggs and incubating them separately, the adult peregrines were stimulated to continue producing eggs," she says. "Up to three batches could be laid in a single season." The natural clutch size is four eggs, meaning a potential of twelve young peregrines that could then be released in the wild.

Data suggest that peregrines can learn to fly and hunt on their own without instruction from an adult falcon. With that knowledge, biologists released thirty-five-day-old chicks in historical nesting places and on skyscrapers in what are known as hack boxes, wooden boxes with screened sides that can be lifted to feed the young, again with peregrine puppets. Rocks are placed in the bottom of the hack boxes to simulate natural nesting sites. Humans continue to watch and feed the peregrines during their time in the hack boxes, until one day, the young emerge to start learning to fly and hunt on their own. The Raptor Center in Minnesota, which coordinates the Midwest programs, provided immature peregrines for the Michigan release sites, where biologists including

Rogers and Kenner hoped the peregrines would return to breed. An important part of the program is checking the release sites each year to see if the captive-bred young come back to nest, and if they are able to lay stronger eggs than their ancestors plagued with DDT contamination laid.

The first hack sites in Michigan were at Isle Royale National Park in 1988, followed by more releases at Pictured Rocks National Lakeshore in 1989. "They were flown in from the Raptor Center," says Kenner. "We picked them up at the airport, then we hiked them in a mile and a half to the hack site. In 1990, a pair showed up on the cliff, so we didn't set young out there because they would be attacked by the pair protecting territory. But in 1991, we had five birds in the first group, five in the next group, and two in the last group. In the box they remain really calm. They're covered with down and look soft to the touch. But you stick your hand in there and they'll grab you with their talons. You have to wear gloves. They're completely unintimidated. When it's time to get them out of the cages to put in a hack box with a screen, you have to reach in, grab their legs, and hang onto them, keeping their wings pinned down."

"You're bringing up this rare animal," says Rogers. "They're little white, fuzzy, downy things. Then you put them in this big cage, a four-by-four-by-six-foot solid-wood and screening hack box, set out on platforms, on a tower fifteen feet tall, twenty-four feet wide, and twenty feet deep. You reach in and grab them as quickly as you can to set them in the hack box. They scream good and loud."

"They get fed quail for a few days with the screen closed," Kenner explains. "After a certain age, the screen gets opened, and then when they're ready to fly, you'll see them on the deck, perching and flapping their wings."

Rogers was hired as a hack-site attendant for a very important reason. A former mountain-climbing trainer for the U.S. Army Eighty-second Airborne Division, Rogers knows how to scale a cliff. Other biologists worked with young peregrines at the top of tall buildings in such places as Chicago and Detroit, where they could take an elevator up to the top and easily reach the hack box. To scale a cliff in the UP requires a unique individual. Indeed, Rogers is. Raised in Michigan, Rogers spent somewhat atypical summers as a youth, going not to softball camps, but to Audubon camps, and not only learning to ski on a trip to Switzerland, but also to climb mountains. When he was only eighteen years old, Rogers rehabilitated his first hawk. Since then he has probably worked with one thousand hawks, peregrine falcons, and eagles in need of his help to save their lives. The seemingly fearless man also enjoys kayaking, canoeing, and spelunking, exploring dark, dank, winding caves, where he has no idea what is around the next turn.

Rogers's education while with the army in the 1970s prepared him for his life with the peregrines. He received military awards for marksmanship, which wife Barb says "comes in handy when your camp is surrounded by bears. Though he's never had to shoot one, it can be reassuring." And when asked at the base of the three-hundred-foot-tall Trap Hills which part of the cliff he couldn't reach, Rogers could honestly answer, "None." And so in 1988, Rogers began camping on the cliffs where the peregrines were hacked so he could watch them constantly. It took him five trips from his car to the site to set up camp. There two volunteers and another paid attendant stayed with him during the three most critical weeks. "You want to protect the baby birds in the tower," says Rogers. "A lot goes on in nature at night." The peregrines needed to be fed daily. Rogers watched as they established a pecking order—who gets to sit where. "They were fighting over the big rocks," he says. "So we got them all big rocks. There were six to eight birds on the same platform in boxes."

Rogers, who has a bachelor's degree in biology from Central Michigan University, is not afraid to express human qualities he thinks he sees in the birds. He's written personality sketches of the juvenile falcons while sitting in a tent, waiting for the rain to stop. There was Zorro, a good flyer but bashful and often the last one to feed; and Steve, a good-sized male who became the parent, allowing the other birds to learn from his success hunting. Ann was the largest and most vocal falcon. She learned to hunt ravens, vultures, and eagles. Sue was the enterprising female who fell off the tower and used a ladder to return to safety.

Rogers is somewhat of a mother hen when it comes to peregrines. He swats flies so they won't lay eggs in the young peregrines' ears where they hatch into maggots. "If it really got bad, we wrapped the bird in a towel and held open the ear and took out the maggots with a pair of tweezers." He did this while hanging over the side of a precipice. "Some people are bothered a lot, standing at the edge of a cliff on top of a tower built out of a few old trees and swaying in the wind," says Rogers. "But I don't mind." He says he's safer there than driving through traffic congestion in heavily populated cities.

While living with the peregrines, Rogers has to protect the birds from various predators, including weasels, raccoons, otters, and hawks. Throwing small rocks discourages the weasels, but Rogers resorts to a more interesting trick to deter bears. In his weekly memo for the Peregrine Release Project, he wrote, "One bear established a rather well-worn trail as it half-circled back and forth about forty feet out from camp almost nightly. It also showed great interest, with paw marks and nose rubs, in that area of the woods behind camp designated as the girls' bathroom. I decided to scent mark, much the same way a dog would, a couple of spots on this bear's trail. The bear, not respecting my dominant role, scratched and tore up, and then pushed and threw around, the areas of dirt and plants that I had marked and remarked the area strongly enough so that I could smell it. I decided to leave the bear and its path alone."

Rogers and other biologists worked for three years picking the sites for the peregrines, analyzing prey species, and making sure the young would have enough to eat. Rogers watched the young learn to become adults. "They slowly learn to fly and to hunt," he says. "They flap their wings. Then they start watching everything more, chasing a leaf or twig, and playing with it like a kitten would play with a ball of string. Males dominate at first, then females get bigger and the pecking order changes. At first we'd feed them every morning so they had energy to go out and hunt. Then we'd see how they would do on their own for one day. Peregrines are intelligent. They follow their parents. They can learn how to hunt from them. But out there with no parents, they had to learn by trial and error. The second year I was up there, a peregrine followed an American kestrel. It would chase the kestrel as it caught grasshoppers. That kestrel almost took on the role of a foster parent." Like the peregrine, the American kestrel is a falcon with streamlined wings for fast maneuvering, but it is half the peregrine's size.

When autumn came, the fully grown peregrines, reacting on instinct, left for the warm weather of Florida and Central and South America, where more food is available. Rogers returned to his winter home, too, wondering if the peregrines would rejoin him in the UP the next spring. Would these peregrines who were hand-raised by humans return to raise young on their own? Impatient for spring and the peregrines' return, Rogers heads back to the UP. He often skis or walks on snowshoes for ten or more miles in late April to see if the peregrines are back. With his slightly stocky build, Rogers might appear to be a bit out of shape. But put him on skis, snowshoes, or in hiking boots, or send him off in a kayak on churning waters, and it's apparent that his stamina and physical abilities could easily outmatch a younger, more muscular-looking man. There's no stopping Joe Rogers when he steps into the outdoors. He is like a boy released on a playground at recess, bounding through the woods. This is his territory—the cliffs of the UP.

"We go up on the cliffs as soon as the snow is off in early May to see if they're flying around," says Brian Kenner, resource management specialist for Pictured Lakes National Lakeshore. "In 1994, the peregrines came back and nested on a historic site at Pictured Rocks. We had our spotting scope and kept good tabs on them. Two fledged, but we found one dead on the beach. A gull had gotten it, and we never found the other one." No peregrines returned to breed at Isle Royale. Rogers guesses the ones released there have found better nesting quarters across the border in Canada. He thinks the peregrines that historically nested on Isle Royale were overflow from Canada, and speculates that if their numbers increase in Canada, peregrines may return to Isle Royale.

Still, just because you can't find them doesn't mean they aren't there. Trying to find a nesting pair of peregrines among the UP's hundreds of miles of bluffs is like searching for a face in a crowd of millions. Rogers attempts to find the birds from every angle. He sits at the top of the cliff, sits at the bottom of the cliff, scales the cliff, and kayaks beside the cliff. One peregrine watcher reported that no falcon had successfully fledged at a particular location, but Rogers kayaked to the site and observed two young peregrines learning how to hunt. He and Barb pack several days' worth of food, camping gear, and their dog in their kayaks, then float out into Lake Superior.

On a calm, sunny day, their kayaks ride the gentle waves like gulls bobbing on water. Offshore, a pair of common loons yodel to one another; the male rises in the water, flaps his wings as if he were ready to fly, then settles back down into the water and circles the female. Storms can come from nowhere out on Lake Superior, and a blustery wind can send waves over a kayaker's head. Portaging along the rugged cliffs offers no security when the rains come. There's nothing to do but ride out the storm.

Rogers also benefits from the help of his friend Bob Sprague, a naturalist at Porcupine Mountains Wilderness State Park. One May day in 1994, Sprague called Rogers to tell him he thought he saw a pair of peregrines. The two birds had chosen a cliff overlooking Lake of the Clouds. Peregrines had not been released there, but this pair had apparently decided it was a good place to breed.

Since then, Rogers has spent hours in spring and summer sitting at the top of the Escarpment Trail, overlooking Lake of the Clouds, watching for peregrines while flies hover over his head and chiggers bite his ankles. "This is a great part of the world," he says. "I grew up with this. I was dragged along bird-watching as a boy. In fact, my mom probably carried me out bird-watching when I was too little to walk. I worked with bird banders in high school. I loved being out in that wild country seeing the wood turtles and lady's tresses." Confined to the northern swamps and woodland streams, the wood turtle, with its subdued brown-and-black markings, is only five to nine inches long, but Rogers can spot it and identify it. He watches bees sip nectar, pollinating the multiple white flowers of the slender-stalked lady's tresses. He knows the serviceberries, which the locals call sugar plums and saskatoons, by their white blossoms in late spring and their pomelike reddish berries of late summer. He finds the creamy yellow flowers of bunchberries in moist woodlands, and the trailing, evergreen bearberry in the rocky escarpments. There's wild sarsaparilla, red osier dogwood, Canada mayflowers, star flowers, and star sedges, twinkling at the top of a wooded cliff. He knows many of the hundreds of plant and animal species here as he would intimate friends. For Joe enjoying nature is more than just something to do while trekking up miles of cliff trails, lugging fifty pounds of gear. It's his silent check that the ecosystem is still working. Rogers has even discovered a rare fern that grows only several inches tall. To protect the species, logging had to be stopped in one area. It pays to get down on your hands and knees, sniff the decaying leaves, and explore the inconspicuous plants emerging from the soil.

Peregrine courtship usually begins in April. The male gets prey and the female gives chase so that he will drop it and she can catch it. When she remains in an area that seems like a good nesting site and lets the male hunt more, she may be on eggs. Both parents share incubation duties. Rogers will not check to see if a nest has eggs until he thinks they are close to hatching, at least two weeks from when he believes they were laid. Eggs hatch in about thirty days. If he approaches too closely early in the nesting cycle, the peregrines could abandon their eggs. "But once they're near hatching and then after hatching, they'll remain even when a human is nearby," he says. They defend the nest at this time with such vigor that "when you check for eggs, you end up with holes in the back of your shirt."

As Rogers looks for peregrines, nature reveals to him its mysteries. In May, migrating broad-winged hawks fly over the Escarpment Trail and the northern goshawk establishes its territory. One spring, as the migrating broad-wings came through, a goshawk bombarded them. The broad-wings tucked their wings in and headed straight for peregrine territory, only to be chased by peregrines directly into a sharp-shinned hawk's chosen nesting site.

"They were screaming and fighting," says Rogers. "And it was beautiful."

Rogers observes these scenes from a little nook at the top of the Escarpment Trail between two scraggly white pine trees. There, away from the overpowering green of the forests, he discovers the more subtle colors of mourning cloaks, white admirals, and other butterflies, searching for what little nectar they can find, then sailing to a more suitable eating place.

Rogers picks up a rock and talks of silver and copper mining in the western UP at the turn of the century. The miners are the reason some of this land has remained virgin forest. They bought forests adjacent to the land they would mine. These woods provided trees for building a home or creating fire for warmth. When the loggers came, the miners wouldn't sell. The state of Michigan bought the land in the 1930s and 1940s and preserved it as park land. "People moved into little cabins here in the 1930s and 1940s to enjoy the wilderness," says Rogers. "Little by little, people developed a wilderness ethic."

A red-eyed vireo and scarlet tanager begin singing as we wait at the top of the cliff for the peregrines. Meanwhile, Rogers has more stories to tell and thoughts to share.

"The official word is that no human has been killed by a bear up here," he says. But then comes the truth according to Joe Rogers: A camper was once chased by a bear into a tree. The bear knocked him out of the tree. "He officially died of a concussion." But, according to Joe, the bear had a bit of a smorgasbord after the man died, leaving only enough to recognize that it indeed was a human.

Then there's the one about the hikers who discovered a pair of boots at an abandoned cabin, ransacked, apparently, by a bear. Inside the boots were the remains of a man's legs. Rogers has the knack of turning legends into what appear to be true stories.

Once, when sleeping in his truck on a ledge near a nesting site, Rogers awakened as the vehicle started to shake. Rogers sat up and looked into two big eyes glaring at him through the window. Two big, black, bear eyes.

"The bear pushed its face through the window," says Rogers. "Then suddenly from behind came another black, furry thing, growling and biting the bear's face." It was Bonnie, Rogers's dog. "Then it was chaos. Here was the bear and Bonnie barking and growling. Then the bear steps back, stands up on its hind legs, Bonnie still growling. And he runs away, Bonnie still with bear fur in her teeth." Bonnie has a nickname now: Bear Bait.

A common raven casts its shadow over Lake of the Clouds. Rogers says he thinks ravens have learned to nest near peregrines for added protection. At Pictured Rocks, he has found peregrine nests by searching for raven nests. At least that is his theory. "You come up with great theories when you sit up here for eighty days," he says.

Finally, it happens. A streamlined bird whizzes by. The male peregrine. He does a figure eight in the air, the female flies out, the male passes her the food, and she takes it back to the nest site. The male is gone. Thirty seconds have passed. You could miss that easily. "That's a good indication they are on eggs," says Rogers. We wait again. "It could be this is the after-dinner shift. Sometimes the male waits for her to finish a meal and bathe in the lake, and then he'll go off to hunt again." And sometimes on a windy day, the feathers of the peregrine's prey litter the entire length of the trail. Rogers thinks the peregrines sometimes stash dead prey in the face of the cliff for a few days—another of his theories, developed during long hours spent at the top of a cliff.

Then the male is back, and the female is screaming at him. He screams back. Then he's gone again. "We might wait another two or three hours for more action," says Rogers. "You can be sitting and reading a book and the bird moves for fifteen seconds, and you may have missed an opportunity, and have to wait another four hours. I've learned not to give up too easily."

A raptor's success depends on food supply. When it's time to feed the young, the adults need a fresh kill every day that provides the nestlings with protein and moisture. The adults also protect the young more when abundant food is available. Otherwise, the nestlings usually don't survive. A late frost or heavy storm can wipe out nesting birds. Even a bad insect year can do it. One year with a late frost, the berries froze. Even the bears were going into town to find food. All the peregrine young died. In 1995, the peregrines lost the first batch of eggs on top of the cliffs near where we are sitting. The female laid a second batch that year around the Fourth of July, but that summer was so hot the eggs cooked.

Nonetheless, the Michigan DNR considers the peregrine release efforts successful, but more so in the cities than in their natural, pre-skyscraper nesting sites. "There are plenty of birds out there," says Brian Kenner. "They're reproducing well. Our habitat is iffy. The cliffs near Lake Superior can be windy, cold."

But Rogers is not calling it a success yet. "Passenger pigeon flocks were once followed by peregrines, but when the flocks were destroyed, when the pigeons became extinct, the peregrines shifted to catching mostly shorebirds. There used to be masses of shorebirds, but not anymore," he says. "Today, the peregrine's prey base is totally different. We need to keep going up there, to see what there is to catch, where they hunt, and identify the nest sites so that if trails are nearby, we can keep people off them for a while or so we can stop planned logging while they're nesting." Mary Hennen of the Chicago Academy of Sciences, however, thinks the peregrine falcon is probably not so species-specific in its choice of prey. "They can get anything up to the size of a small duck," she says. Both scientists, however, appreciate how vital identifying prey species is to the preservation of peregrines. Protecting habitat and minimizing human impact are two other important factors. Naturalist Bob Sprague gladly rerouted the major trail system at the Porcupine Mountains when peregrines chose to breed there. Humans were getting too close to the nest site.

"We don't expect the peregrines to come back like the eagles," says Rogers. "There were ten peregrine pairs nesting in Michigan in 1998 and 250 bald eagle pairs. At one time, there were less than fifty pairs of eagles nesting in the state."

"There is an anti-peregrine sentiment out here," says Rogers. People kill them. Twenty dead raptors were discovered recently, possibly killed by people thinking the birds were peregrines, says Rogers. "People go out of their way to run over a dead hawk, whether it's a peregrine or a red-shouldered hawk or another species, on the road," he says. "It's a symbol that they want to kill the peregrines." Some hunters think peregrines are depleting the ruffed grouse population. So they shoot the peregrines.

But biologists like Joe Rogers who understand how peregrines hunt know that isn't true. He has enlisted the help of grade-school and high-school students from Michigan, who, among other things, sold homemade cards adorned with hand-pressed flowers to raise funds for radio equipment. The radios enable Rogers to space volunteers and interns along the cliffs where they can converse with each other about where the peregrines are and what they are eating. The research enabled Rogers to learn that "in the Porkies, the peregrines are hunting more like merlins and other accipiters. They're getting downy woodpeckers, juncos, cedar waxwings, and occasionally Forster's terns. They're working hard to get prey."

Rogers also wonders if the birds born in the wild are "chemically dirty. The parents in the hacking program were raised clean. But once the young have gone into the wild and grown up, are they clean enough to produce young? DDT is still used in other countries," he says. "Migrating birds that ingest the DDT in those countries return to the United States to breed in the summer, and become peregrine prey. DDT is still affecting the peregrines." That is why banding the chicks and observing their behavior if and when they return to their nesting sites as adults is an important part of the release and restoration program.

Rogers thinks the peregrine falcon should not be removed from the Federal Endangered Species List, even though the U.S. Fish and Wildlife Service recommended that be done in August 1999. Rogers says although a few harmful pesticides have been banned in the United States, many of the contaminants remain in the environment and are still hindering the recovery of some populations. As of 1990, in California high levels of DDE (a derivative of DDT) contamination still existed. The sources of contamination vary, but one was an insecticide that was still used in the Central Valley, according to the Endangered Species Recovery Program in Fresno, California.

The Peregrine Fund, however, supports the removal of the peregrine falcon from the list of endangered and threatened species, even though not all of the specific recovery goals of the five recovery plans have been precisely attained, says founding chairman Tom Cade.

There are several peregrine falcon subspecies that some say should stay on the endangered species list. But Cade says, "When the subspecies is viewed as a continental population, it quite clearly no longer meets the definition of endangered or threatened as given in the Endangered Species Act." Cade says overall population trends, higher reproductive rates, and decreasing levels of pesticide residues in the environment bode well for the peregrine falcon.

Some people worry that 1,593 known breeding pairs is too small a number to consider safe, adds Cade, but naturally rare species like the peregrine are adapted to survive and maintain stable numbers at very low densities and small total population sizes.

Cade says the use of DDT and other chemicals that harm peregrines have been restricted or eliminated in North America since the 1970s, and residues in the environment and in prey animals have declined greatly since the 1980s. He admits that though local hot spots of high concentrations exist, and eggshell thinning still affects some populations of peregrines at near-critical levels, most peregrine populations have shown increased eggshell thickness. He predicts that environmental residues of DDE and related compounds will further decay, and eggshell thickness will continue to increase.

Cade says a well-executed and adequately funded five-year post-delisting monitoring program is particularly important for the peregrine because of the great public interest in this species.

But Joe Rogers and Mary Hennen fear the public will lose interest in this bird and that the delisting will prohibit any more funding for important research projects needed to ensure the health of the peregrine falcon.

So Rogers will keep climbing.

One of Rogers's favorite cliffs to climb in the UP is in the Trap Hills. "It's a three-hundred-foot vertical rock," he says, not with fear, not with awe, just as a statement of fact. Actually Trap Hills is a series of rocks, some of them as large as a two-car garage. The rocks appear monstrous to an unskilled climber, but while I'm dreading the climb, in fact, determined that I will not climb, Rogers is talking about the thrill of watching a storm develop here.

"Some beautiful storms come in at times," he says. "You just find a place to hide along the side of a hill." Today, it is sunny and warm, and Rogers leads us along unmarked trails surrounded by green—hemlocks, spruces, maples, and other deciduous trees. You'd swear you're headed north, only to discover by looking at your compass that you're walking south. The fear of being lost dissolves into a sense of wonder when Rogers talks.

"Stand here and just look," he says. "This is the closest you will ever get to seeing how North America looked before the settlers came. These are the old-growth hemlocks, the unlogged areas, off the trails. You can feel it, see it, smell it, touch it."

And if you make it to the top, you can maybe find a peregrine.

Across from some old, shattered railroad ties, Joe Rogers sits and stares at the Trap Hills, the day after he discovered there were no eggs at the nest site in the Porcupine Mountains. He did not see any peregrines at Trap Hills when he visited the area three weeks ago. He watches the cliffs now, telling his stories again. He rescued a biologist once who thought he was well-versed in mountain climbing, that is until he came to the Trap Hills and lost his footing among the jagged edges of these huge, ancient rocks. The biologist spent an hour dangling from ropes while Rogers devised the plan that would return the man to safety. Rogers has helped save the lives of several people researching birds in the western UP or hiking through the backwoods. He has taught young interns how to survive in the woods, how to properly climb a mountain, how to be careful when working with peregrines, and how to avoid falling into an old mine shaft. One person a year ventures into these woods and is never found again, says Rogers.

EEEEEEEEEEEEEEEEEE.

"There she is!"

Hope rises in his voice like a broad-winged hawk rising on a thermal. Rogers aims his scope on a site at the top of a cliff. "There's the nest," he says. He sees a female's head barely visible inside the small, cavelike structure on the cliff above a vegetated rock outcrop.

EEEEEEE. EEEEEEEEEEEEEEEE.

"Here comes the male."

The male peregrine performs the requisite aerial figure eights like an ice-skater in the sky, then is off on the hunt.

Several turkey vultures play games in the wind above the Trap Hills. They ride the current holding their black wings in the typical V shape, skirting an issue—dare they venture into the peregrines' territory? They decide to keep their distance from the peregrine nest site. After all, the female's mate could be nearby, ready to attack. And Joe Rogers, the man who will climb mountains to save the peregrines, is watching guard from below.

Yellow-rumped Warbler

Songs Running Deep

WIND PELTS THE WINDOWPANES of an old Coast Guard station several hundred feet from Lake Superior's shore in the eastern Upper Peninsula. The fog is so thick that no one standing on the shore could see the small building, that is if anyone would be found at this seemingly forsaken place. To get there, you must drive down washboard roads through pine forests and occasional marshy clearings. Dips and mud holes threaten to trap a vehicle at every bend. No one would discover you here for days, maybe weeks. And no one, it seems, is here to appreciate the hermit thrush's haunting trills or the lady slipper's ballerina-pink and white hues.

But someone is here—a lanky, bristle-faced man holding a cup of coffee, a pen, and a clipboard.

Tick-tick-tick-tick. Tickety Tickety Tickety.

"NAWA," Walter Johansen writes on a gridded sheet, standing next to alders at the edge of a sedge meadow.

Quick-three-beers.

"OSFL," Johansen writes.

Johansen is hearing the mating songs of the Nashville warbler (NAWA) and olive-sided flycatcher (OSFL), two songbirds that migrate through and breed in the UP. He records the birds he hears and sees along a specific route beginning at dawn several times a day during late May and June. Other researchers walk other routes in remote areas in Ottawa National Forest, the Porcupine Mountains, the Keweenaw Peninsula, the Huron Mountains—forested areas where songbirds breed or pause for food during migration. These researchers want to know if certain songbird species that migrate through or breed in the UP are declining, and if so, why and how they can be saved.

Johansen and other songbird banders live seasonally at the old Coast Guard station, now the Vermilion bird-banding station, several miles east of Whitefish Point. Each one relishes the experience: no running water, no telephone. A battery-operated pump draws water from a well. A generator keeps batteries charged. It can be cold, damp, and foggy here even on a mid-July day. At dawn, when the work begins, insects abound. Larvae in the wetland pools are developing into mosquitos by the hundreds even as Johansen stands there and records birds for the required ten minutes before moving on to the next stop.

This is how life rings true for the Illinois native, who still lives in his hometown of Villa Park when he's not on the UP. Watching cliff swallows build their mud nests in his backyard and seeing the yellow- and black-hued evening grosbeaks as frequently as one might see a pigeon in the city may well be enough to keep Johansen in this isolated domain year-round. He knows, however, as every UP researcher knows, that is not possible. There are bills to pay, funds to raise, enough so you can maybe come back and do what you love next year and perhaps the year after that.

Upper Peninsula researchers like Johansen are gathering data to help solve a worldwide puzzle with many complex, interlocking pieces. The puzzle is the plight of the neotropical migrants, birds that spend winters in Central and South America, then fly north in spring to breed in North America, many of them in Upper Michigan and Canada. Scientists estimate that more than one-half of all North American bird species migrate south to neotropical zones. Some five billion songbirds migrate south every fall to faraway places, including Argentina, Colombia, and Mexico, then fly north as far as Alaska to breed. These tiny, colorfully feathered creatures weigh less than a half ounce; yet they withstand strong winds and heavy rains as they cross bodies of water such as the Gulf of Mexico. Each bird endures long, exhausting trips that require stops to refuel in places where vegetative shelter guards from predators. Nashville warblers, palm warblers, blackburnian warblers, veeries, Swainson's thrushes, blue-headed vireos, olive-sided flycatchers, and other songbirds find Michigan's UP, with its copious insect life and tracts of uninterrupted forest, a perfect place to nest or refuel before continuing their journey even farther north.

For the last decade or more, fewer of these migrants have been returning to their summer nesting grounds. Some populations of these insectivorous species, including flycatchers, vireos, warblers, thrushes, and tanagers, are declining. In Michigan, populations of at least forty neotropical migrant species, including the rose-breasted grosbeak, golden-winged warbler, and cerulean warbler, are declining. Scientists suggest that increasing development along these birds' migration routes, as well as the destruction of large tracts of forests where they breed, has left them more vulnerable to predation at the same time they are finding it more difficult to locate good food sources.

The researchers who spend hours and days in deep solitude within these woods are finding that certain forestry practices—for example, selective cutting instead of clear-cutting—may maintain a more diverse forest with more habitat for a wider variety of neotropical migrants. The forest is ever changing, however, and decisions about how to manage the woods for the birds and other wildlife will continue to be difficult to make.

No one knows this better than the researchers who suddenly lose their funding to political brouhahas and governmental priority swings. Striking a balance between the priorities of biologists, foresters, and others can be difficult, but researchers believe it can be done. Johansen has worked for several years to determine the migratory patterns of songbirds near the Lake Superior shoreline. Most recently he collaborated with Frances M. Danek, and William Scharf, former director of Whitefish Point Bird Observatory, to gather extensive data on migration pathways, stopover times, and habitat associations of birds in the Whitefish Peninsula, a fifteen-square-kilometer triangle of land that the Michigan Department of Natural Resources manages in Lake Superior State Forest. This land, abutting Whitefish Bay and Lake Superior, supports jack pines, red pines, white pines, tamaracks, black spruce, and small stands of paper birches and other northern hardwoods among swamps, open bogs, sedge wetlands, and small lakes. Regional and global groups, including the Michigan DNR, Whitefish Point Bird Observatory, the Ontario Ministry of Natural Resources, and the World Wildlife Fund, funded the work.

In May and then again in August and September, Johansen and other banders take turns setting up several banding nets behind the Vermilion station to track numbers and species of migrants. Banders also work at Whitefish Point in fall, gathering data on songbird migrants. Several years of data prove how essential the Lake Superior and Whitefish Bay shorelines and adjacent lands are for migrants. "The closer you get to Lake Superior's shoreline, the more migrants you find," says Johansen.

The birds use the lake as a landmark. As they follow the shoreline, they are attracted to the woods that harbor the insects they need for survival. Certain areas near the Coast Guard station are huge migrant pockets. One mid-May day, Johansen watched hundreds of tiny, colorful birds stop to feed in a stand of trees for four hours before flying across Lake Superior to Canada. They wore their bold breeding apparel of nature's finest colors, resembling pointillistic dots on a green canvas as they descended on the trees. Here Johansen witnessed a show to rival any art gallery opening: hundreds of birds displaying black-and-white stripes, golden wing bars, rust-colored caps, jet black throats, russet cheek patches, orange-and-black tails, green backs, orange breast streaks, white eye rings, and black masks.

These small land birds migrate at night, probably to avoid predators such as hawks, which migrate during the day. Scientists believe that nocturnal migrants use the stars as well as shorelines and other landmarks to guide them to their nesting grounds. Attempting to cross open water with insufficient fat storage can be suicidal. That is why areas such as Whitefish Peninsula, which juts out into the bay and lake, as well as the Keweenaw Peninsula in the western UP, are so important. Migratory songbirds are trapped here on their way north until they can add the necessary fat to their bodies to fly farther. These birds find the best food about a half mile to a mile or so away from shore. While banding and recapturing spring migrants in these areas, Johansen and other researchers discovered a golden-crowned kinglet that had gained 13 percent of its body weight in one day, supporting the theory that nocturnal migrants may be able to fatten enough in one day for a flight the next day. Most of the migrants remained in wet, mixed-forest habitat; hardly any used clear-cuts or regenerating clear-cuts. The food and protection from predators are just not there.

A report prepared in 1997 for Whitefish Point Bird Observatory tells the story precisely. Cutting mature trees will eliminate food sources for nocturnal migrants. And that could mean "massive mortality during migration due to starvation and the inability to evade predators." The report's recommendations are equally straightforward. "The Lake Superior State Forest lands within 1.6 kilometers (about one mile) of both shorelines of the Whitefish Peninsula should be protected from extensive timber harvesting and development." The recent addition of some of this land—approximately twenty acres—to the National Wildlife Refuge system as well as the establishment by a private landowner of the Wild Shore Foundation near the Vermilion banding station may afford the migratory birds some protection.

Other Michigan research adds credence to the report's findings. Dave Ewert, a biologist and director of science and stewardship with the Michigan Nature Conservancy, and his colleagues have spent several years researching bird migration and feeding patterns along Lake Huron. They found that midges, a family of insects that number in the hundreds of thousands along the lakeshore, attract birds there during spring migration. Ewert says scientists now understand more clearly the intricate relationships between food sources, birds, and habitats. They know that songbirds help maintain a forest's health by devouring many insects that might otherwise harm trees.

The presence of the blackburnian warbler, a neotropical migrant, may serve as a signal to land managers that a forest is healthy. The Michigan DNR is monitoring nesting blackburnian warblers one hundred miles southwest of the Vermilion banding station. This five-inch-long bird with a fiery orange throat and white wing patch winters in South America, but when spring comes, it migrates to Michigan, Wisconsin, the New England states, the Appalachian Mountains, and Canada to breed, choosing mature upland conifers for its summer home. "We are using the blackburnian warbler as an indicator species," says Robert Doepker, the wildlife biologist leading the study. The blackburnian warbler serves as a sort of surrogate representing other animal and plant species that need similar habitats in which to live and propagate.

Tsip Tsip Tsip Titi Zeeeeee, the male blackburnian calls in a soft, sibilant voice. He may be called a warbler, but he doesn't warble and he doesn't sing. He rather enunciates several lisplike syllables barely within a human's range of hearing. But what he lacks in voice, the blackburnian warbler surely makes up in color. No other plant or animal in nature so clearly defines the color "orange" as the male blackburnian warbler with his sun-kissed throat contrasting with a black-striped head and black eye line and cheek patch. Every birder in Texas, Illinois, Michigan, Iowa, or anywhere along the bird's migratory path, rejoices when his or her binoculars focus on the male blackburnian warbler. The less-brilliant female, nearly named a different species by John James Audubon, builds her nest alone, gathering plant down, twigs, spider silk, and fine grasses from the ground, then bringing the material to a small fork near the top of a hemlock, pine, fir, spruce, or occasionally an oak. The female tucks her nest into the densest, highest part of the tree, where it cannot be seen from the ground. She lays her four to five eggs sometime in May or June; the young hatch in only eleven to twelve days and can fly another eleven or twelve days after that. While in the nest, male and female bring the young plenty of caterpillars, ants, beetles, and other insect morsels. By the time autumn comes, the young join their parents and other warblers of various species in their first migratory flight south, where the insects they need continue to proliferate during the northern winter. Many of the UP's nesting warblers, flycatchers, vireos, tanagers, and thrushes follow the same pattern, each choosing different niches in which to build their nests and feed their young but all relying on copious insects for survival.

You won't find the blackburnian warbler on any threatened or endangered species list, but the research being done in the UP is still important. It is proactive research, as opposed to the reactive research scientists were forced to perform when eagle and peregrine falcon numbers declined so dramatically. Scientists aren't waiting to see if a neotropical migrant bird species declines to the point where it should be listed as a threatened species; they are studying them now, making sure they know what these birds need to survive. It's a difficult task because even though as a whole the number of neotropical migrants appears to be decreasing, some of the species' numbers are stable and some are even increasing. Knowing more about the birds' wintering as well as breeding habitat can help scientists better understand the population dynamics of neotropical migrants and be better prepared if something goes awry. The acreage of mature conifers in the UP where the blackburnian warbler nests has declined approximately 75 percent from presettlement conditions, says Doepker, and that could be affecting the warbler.

It's important to understand the history of lumbering in the UP, and to be careful not to blame the deforestation on just one industry or company. In the 1910s and 1920s, timber companies heavily harvested the UP's white and red pines and shipped them for use in the growing cities of Chicago and Detroit. The great cities of the Great Lakes were built, in fact, from UP forests. To get harvested timber to its destination, workers dug ditches and channelized streams and wetlands, which along with extensive lumbering denuded many parts of the UP. After the logging was done, the UP smoldered with wildfires, because loggers left behind extremely volatile slash, or waste. Once the wildfires abated, secondary growth began. Today, a rich resource still exists in the UP's forests for the paper and pulp industry. Softwoods such as red and white pine can be processed and used for paper to produce books like the one you are reading.

Humans learn lessons from the past—and that is precisely why at 5 A.M. in late May and throughout June, Doepker and his research assistant, Andrew Watkins, hop in a green pickup truck and drive out to the forests to listen for blackburnian warblers. Tall, lanky, dark-haired, and cleanly shaven, Watkins wears a T-shirt, jeans, and hiking boots. Young and yet wise about the constant struggle between humans and the environment, Watkins walks among the hemlocks, basswoods, and other trees, noting how many blackburnian warblers are singing and holding territories. Doepker, the more experienced biologist of the two, with a quiet, scholarly demeanor, walks the perimeter of the study area using a global positioning system (GPS) unit. The GPS receives satellite data that help Doepker determine the exact location of forest stand territories. Hiking through a forest floor laden with maple and beech saplings and Canada mayflower, Watkins plucks ticks from his clothes and tosses them back onto the forest floor. Doepker just walks.

The stand of trees where they walk is suitable breeding habitat for the blackburnian warbler. It's an area that hasn't been cut yet, on private property owned by a paper manufacturing company. "We compare the information from this control group with randomly selected sites that are being harvested in the UP," says Watkins.

Modern-day technology gives them access to remarkable data. The technology comes from U.S. government–owned satellites circling Earth. "Using these satellites, you can pinpoint your location on the surface of Earth," says Watkins. He and Doepker use that information along with satellite imagery to determine the types of plant species and number of forested acres in an area. Then they estimate the amount of breeding habitat suitable for blackburnians. The ultimate goal is to identify suitable blackburnian habitat and then work with foresters to manage some of the landscape for this warbler and other wildlife species associated with mature upland conifers, says Doepker. Data suggest that blackburnian warblers prefer mature, upland conifers of hemlock, white pine, balsam fir, white spruce, and natural stands of red pine. Doepker emphasizes the word *natural* because "we have not located blackburnian warblers in pine plantations." State and federal governments and timber companies plant red pines, typically in rows, to reforest the UP in some areas because they grow quickly and also provide softwood for the paper industry.

Optimal blackburnian nesting sites are forest stands containing approximately 75 percent conifers and 25 percent deciduous trees of large diameter. "Blackburnians spend considerable time foraging in deciduous trees," says Doepker. So the species needs a mix of trees in which to breed and feed.

While doing his research, Doepker uses his birding ears to the fullest. He has learned to recognize two distinct blackburnian warbler breeding songs—a soft, wheezy song and a buzzier, more piercing call. The blackburnian is not the only bird singing in the woods, of course. Walking through the forest, Doepker can also hear the abundant black-throated green warbler, the Nashville warbler, and the American redstart. *Zoo Zee Zoo Zoo Zee* sings the black-throated green warbler. *See-weet-see-weet-see-weet, trilllllll* adds the Nashville warbler, with yellow body, blue head, and white eye ring. Chiming in with its series of high, thin, varibale notes exploding at the end is the American redstart, called the butterfly of the warbler world because it fans a gorgeous red-and-black tail. Put them all together and you hear a pleasant riot of sound.

Recognizing birdsong is a requirement of research on neotropical migrants. How else could you find the blackburnian warbler, which builds its nest fifty to sixty feet high? Or the ovenbird, which builds a well-camouflaged, dome-shaped nest of grasses and woody stems lined with deer hair on the ground? With its streaked breast and brownish orange crown, the ovenbird melds with the debris on the forest floor, remaining undetected by the casual observer. Instead, birders listen for the ovenbird's ringing *Teacher Teacher Teacher* call echoing through the woods.

It's not just birdsong that has endeared Doepker to his chosen life's work for more than twenty-five years. It's his fascination with how plants and animals work together. "That has intrigued me for a long time," says Doepker, a father of two who grew up in a southern Michigan farming community where he fished, hunted pheasant, and hiked through the woods. He studied technical drafting and tool design his first two semesters in college. "But I realized that type of occupation was not right for me," he says. So he switched to biology, earning a bachelor's and a master's degree.

Doepker's first job after college was what some might call a "pay-your-dues job." He, like many young college graduates, worked as a temporary employee for the U.S. Fish and Wildlife Service and the Michigan Department of Natural Resources on Michigan and Wisconsin wildlife refuges. He observed hunter behavior, mowed dikes, hazed geese, banded waterfowl, and trapped and relocated wild turkeys. Doepker then got an opportunity to study the endangered Kirtland's warbler in Lower Michigan. "We worked on a habitat assessment project, predicting where the Kirtland's warbler might nest by using the combination of tree species composition, soils, and other factors," he says. "That's the kind of work that really interested me." Finally, Doepker was offered a permanent job with the Michigan DNR near Norway, Michigan, where he has been for twenty years.

"It's more laid back" says Doepker about living in a small town in the UP. "There's not a lot of culture." His two children, Katie and Robbie, have received a good education there, and he has been able to work at what he loves. Doepker now monitors and assesses wildlife and their habitats across the UP. The information he and his coworkers gather enables resource managers to improve their decision making. "The approach is called ecosystem management," says Doepker. "It's a more holistic approach, integrating biological, ecological, and social data that land managers and wildlife ecologists can use when managing all resources in forested systems."

Mike Mossman, a wildlife researcher for the Wisconsin Department of Natural Resources, is also studying the effects of forest management on breeding songbirds and small mammals, salamanders, and frogs. He, too, knows the songs of the ovenbird, the blackburnian warbler, and some one hundred other songbirds documented as breeding in Michigan's UP and northern Wisconsin. Like Doepker, Mossman also spent his early years as a biologist working temporary jobs and not knowing if he'd be working the next year or not.

Now a permanent Wisconsin DNR employee, Mossman is comparing three types of forests: fragments of old-growth forests, or areas that have never been cut; even-aged forests that have been clear-cut; and uneven-aged forests that have been selectively cut. "There are not many old-growth reference sites in Wisconsin, or even the nation," says Mossman. "But there are some left in the UP." So to make comparisons, he spent several summers researching songbirds in the wildest areas of the UP, in the Sylvania Wilderness Area near Norway, the Porcupine Mountains, and portions of Ottawa National Forest. Mossman began his study by walking transects or straight lines through many forested areas, stopping for five minutes every four hundred meters to record all birds he heard or saw. This provided preliminary data on the species, numbers, and distribution of birds breeding in various forests, those manipulated by humans and those not. Mossman then worked with Robert Howe of the University of Wisconsin in Green Bay and a team of field-workers to study breeding-bird densities and reproductive success for two summers on plots selected to represent each forest type.

This work is part of a cooperative, multidisciplinary study by the Wisconsin DNR and the University of Wisconsin to study the effects of management on the forest ecology of northern Wisconsin and the adjacent UP. "It's an exciting project," says Mossman. "We use the same set of study sites to research everything from soils and nutrient cycling to mushrooms, insects, birds, mammals, and the structure of the forest itself."

Mossman and several other biologists camped in the Sylvania Wilderness and the Porcupine Mountains, backpacking up to cabins and Adirondack shelters. "You can walk for hours and not run into roads, logged areas, or other unnatural disturbances," says Mossman. "You can get immersed in it. You can get lost in there. It's a great feeling. In the Porkies, we commonly found chimney swifts, a bird that probably would have gone extinct had it not been for chimneys. They need big hollow trees, with a fairly wide diameter, and broken off at the top like a chimney. It has a different meaning when you see the chimney swifts out there in the wild."

If you happen to see Mossman in the wild, you will meet a friendly, full-bearded man—after all there's no extra room in the backpack for nonessentials like a razor—whose encouraging voice espouses hope for the songbirds. Long, dark, wavy hair is kept off his forehead with a bandana. His wife, Lisa Hartman, who sometimes accompanies him, keeps her hair tucked neatly in a tied-back scarf. She wears overalls and a long-sleeved shirt on a mid-September day in Gogebic County, Michigan, as they perform another important part of Mossman's work—recording trees' circumference, height, and other data necessary to determine which sizes and types of trees and understory vegetation songbirds need to reproduce successfully. Mossman says he enjoys working in the fall in the UP almost better than in the spring and summer. "It's gorgeous. The colors. The smells of the leaf mold. The soft rains for days. The chilly air. And no bugs. It's great," he says. "But just wear wool." When autumn comes, the temperatures plummet.

Mossman is used to this cold northern air. Born and raised in a small Wisconsin town, he enjoyed hiking outdoors in the forested bluffs and stream gorges of the Baraboo Hills more than he enjoyed going to school.

His father, an Iowa native, moved the family to Wisconsin where Mossman immediately immersed himself into the world of Boy Scouts and camping trips. For his seventeenth birthday his father gave him not a new car, but rather a copy of Aldo Leopold's *A Sand County Almanac*, which Mossman says changed his life.

Mossman recalls getting pledges to collect garbage from the bluffs and the Baraboo River on Earth Day in 1971, when he was a high school senior. The students dumped the garbage they collected on the high school parking lot to "make a statement," he says. Mossman said he never got along with the principal, and the garbage-dumping episode did not improve their relationship. But Mossman did get along with his biology teacher, Gerald Scott, who urged his students to go out in the field and study birds, plants, and mammals. Mossman and his fellow activist students donated the money they raised from collecting garbage on Earth Day to The Nature Conservancy, which used the money toward buying forty acres of forest in an isolated stream gorge called Pan Hollow near Mossman's home. The students dedicated the preserve to Mr. Scott.

Mossman then earned a bachelor's degree in zoology education and a master's degree in wildlife ecology, even though he says he never learned to enjoy school. His first ten years out of college, he worked as a temporary employee for the Wisconsin DNR on research assignments. In 1987, the department offered him a permanent job. Now he works with his wife from his Wisconsin home.

Today, Mossman calls himself a scientist, not an activist, but you can hear the activist spirit in his voice when he talks about the data he is gathering in the UP. "Although no bird species are found solely in old-growth forest, the old-growth community has specific groups of birds, assemblages you find nowhere else in the Great Lakes Region, if not the nation," he says. His voice grows enthusiastic. "You see how things have operated for eons, where birds fit in, and how they have evolved in their habitat preferences. In old-growth forests, the hemlock, sugar maples, and yellow birches have reproduced over time without unnatural disturbance." Downed trees leave coarse, woody debris on the forest floor with rotting logs providing shelter for winter wrens and other species. "The winter wren has one of the most beautiful songs of all birds," says

Mossman. A shy, secretive, brown bird with a short, uplifted tail, it broadcasts a series of melodious tinklings within and without the human range of hearing. You can't get much closer to heaven than standing in a mixed forest in the UP inhaling the incense of decaying pine needles and hearing the winter wren sing. Like a Cheshire cat, it blends into the forest as it probes for insects beneath the scattered logs. But its complex, melodious vocalizations tingle your skin, bore through your soul, and make you feel a part of its universe.

More songs, chatters, buzzes, and flutelike trills emanate from the old-growth forests as Mossman walks his route. Northern parula sing *ZZZZZZZZZZZippp*. Yellow-rumped warblers repeat one fast, high note. Golden-crowned kinglets sing four soft syllables. Swainson's thrushes beckon with their Pan-like whistles and trills.

"These birds characterize healthy hemlock forests," says Mossman. And scientists and forestry managers have been recording a disappearance of hemlocks from the forest canopy. The mathematics is easy: fewer hemlocks equals fewer golden-crowned kinglets, fewer Swainson's thrushes, fewer blackburnian warblers.

Mossman links the loss of hemlocks to deer over-browsing, forest management, and possibly climate. Mossman, however, remains optimistic. Properly managed forests can provide lumber and paper for people as well as nesting sites for birds, he says. The uneven-aged stands or selectively cut forests he examines contain many of the same birds he found in undisturbed old-growth forests. The black-throated blue warbler and the veery, a tawny-brown thrush, for instance, "seem to like areas where there are blowdowns, where canopy trees weakened by fungus were tipped over by the wind, thus letting in light for maple seedlings to grow," says Mossman. This process happens naturally in untouched forests, but humans can mimic it with proper forestry techniques. They can manage unevenly cut areas to provide habitat for the black-throated blue warbler, veery, and other species.

"That's the big challenge now, how to manage the whole landscape," says Mossman. "The National Forest Service and the Wisconsin Department of Natural Resources are interested in doing this. It's a dynamic dance, working with politics, the forest service, the biologists. Answers are not black and white." The forest and its inhabitants change yearly, and not all trends are disturbing. For example, harvested forests that are allowed to regenerate attract species such as mourning warblers and chestnut-sided warblers, birds that require second-growth areas for nesting.

Mossman and other researchers now are working in forty-six study sites in Sylvania Wilderness Area and Ottawa National Forest in the UP. They gather data on birds, forest herb layers, soils, carbon nutrient cycling, beetles, mushrooms, lichens, and amphibians. They are trying to define how the hemlock-hardwood forests work in the UP.

Susan Andres, who also studies breeding songbirds in the UP, is another of the many researchers contributing to our understanding of how the UP forest ecosystems work. Andres, former president of the Copper County Audubon Society, lived from 1986 to 1998 on the Keweenaw Peninsula at the northwesternmost edge of the UP. A pink-cheeked, soft-spoken woman with windblown brown hair, Andres grew up in a farming area near Wheaton, Illinois, which she says has since become just another sprawling Chicago suburb. "Living in the Keweenaw," she says, "is like living on an island in an ocean where there is plenty of wilderness to explore."

Andres and her former husband, Dana Richter, built a home in a quiet, unpopulated area surrounded by woods near Hancock, Michigan. Andres wants people to know that life can be remarkably satisfying in the Keweenaw, even during the hard, cold winters. "We grew our own vegetables, ate simply, and took care of eighty acres surrounding our home," says Andres. They planted more than one thousand trees, mainly conifers, and also established a nature trail through forty acres of aspen, birch, and oak woods behind their home. "Every few years we saw one or two new bird species setting up territory on our land," says Andres. "We shared our abundant *Amelanchier* (serviceberry) crop with the bears, cedar waxwings, and other birds. Mountain ash and wild apple trees attracted occasional wintering robins and other, more northerly winter visitors." Andres also built and erected twenty-five nest boxes that attracted bluebirds, tree swallows, chickadees, kestrels, flickers, phoebes, and house wrens.

"Our small home had large picture windows that provided a constant view of nature happenings. We watched no TV. Instead we found the natural world around us to be our greatest inspiration in life. Spring was never more refreshing than it was then. I could set aside my normal sleep schedule to awaken before the first birdsong of the day and be out at my first station to learn who would be nesting in the woods I called home. Northern Michigan has its long winters, but without winters I could hardly look forward to the annual spring migration. My spirit was renewed as the woods and streams of the Keweenaw abounded with insects, leaves, and birds."

Although Andres doesn't like to admit it, she once wanted to become a fashion designer. But a field ecology course at College of DuPage in Illinois changed her mind. She was not going to fashion-design school; she was going to Minnesota to study biology at St. Cloud State.

"It is hard to say I have chosen this work because I have never really been able to support myself on it," she says. "Luckily, my work at home combined with the support from my spouse enables me to immerse myself in this passion ever so briefly during the spring and summer bird-breeding seasons." Sometimes she gets paid, sometimes she volunteers. Always, she approaches the task with scientific vigor and an intense dedication.

Like Mike Mossman, Andres understands that the issue of songbirds and forestry practice has many sides. But she does believe that if a large-enough area is left undisturbed it has the potential to attract a diverse population of breeding birds and contribute to the health of a forest's ecosystem. That belief comes from her studies of breeding songbirds three miles from Copper Harbor in part of a 377-acre, old-growth forest called the Estivant Pines Nature Sanctuary.

Owned by the Michigan Nature Association, this sanctuary represents a transitional zone between Canada's boreal forests and the deciduous forests of the eastern United States. White pines, some 165 feet tall and 3 feet or more in diameter, grow among northern hardwoods and boreal species such as white spruce and balsam fir. The trails are rough; downed wood from decaying trees covers the forest floor. Randomly scattered rocks and intermittent creeks are welcome interruptions to a woods where trees grow so close together that the forest floor is bare of vegetation. No mechanized vehicles are allowed or could even get through. If you wander off the trail, you need a compass and maps to find your way back.

Amid the pines and hemlocks, Andres chooses her steps well as she walks across fallen logs, into and out of sudden dips in the terrain, and weaves through mud. She records the names of birds singing in the same territory throughout the breeding season. She calculates territory distances and plots a map to show where the birds were. It is hard, dirty, detailed, exhausting work.

And it is exhilarating.

Alone in the woods, with only the sounds of the birds and the wind whispering through leaves, Andres records her data. She listens to the buzzy call of the black-throated blue warbler and the short-phrased *chanson* of the red-eyed vireo, a bird once recorded singing twenty-one thousand times within ten hours. She hears the scarlet tanager's hoarse robinlike song and the eastern wood-pewee call out its name in slurring, liquidy tones. She hears the mellifluous, melancholy aria of the rose-breasted grosbeak; the short, strident *chebek* of the least flycatcher; the *pleased-to-meetcha* chant of the chestnut-sided warbler; the haunting, flutelike tones of the hermit thrush; even the territorial *ki-lick* of the yellow-bellied flycatcher, an uncommon UP breeder that winters in Mexico and Panama but somehow makes it to this remote, northwestern corner of Michigan. Andres's studies yielded a total of 191 individuals of up to fifty-two different species during the breeding season in the old-growth pines sanctuary. As many as 91 percent of those are neotropical migrants.

Following the Estivant Pines research, Andres began working with the U.S. Forest Service and the Michigan Department of Natural Resources to study four areas, each managed differently, in a sugar maple–basswood forest in the western UP's Ottawa National Forest. She studied an unmanaged old-growth plot, a managed old-growth plot that retained some snags and canopy trees reminiscent of old-growth areas, a selectively cut area with small openings that still contained some of the old-growth forest's layered structure, and a thirty-year-old, even-aged stand, which she says "looks more like a park than a forest."

Just as Mossman did, Andres found that the old-growth and selectively cut areas yielded the highest diversity of breeding bird species. In 1994, only thirteen species of birds with 26 different territories used the even-aged plot, while twenty-three species used the old-growth and selectively cut areas. In the old-growth forest, Andres recorded 110 different territories. In the selectively cut areas, she recorded 100. Andres also searched for nests and only found half as many in the selectively cut areas as in the old-growth areas. She says she needs more data to determine patterns. She also wants to examine nest success more closely and analyze insect productivity in the four plots to learn if that determines where the breeding birds choose to nest.

Andres is also now surveying birds that nest in the Huron Mountains, where Dana Richter conducts mycological research. A unique private holding, the Huron Mountains comprises twenty thousand acres, eight thousand of which are designated as a reserve area, never to be developed. "This property is closed to the public, and all research proposals are screened by the Huron Mountain Wildlife Foundation," she says. "I feel very fortunate to be able to explore and survey Huron Mountain birds, as these lands are much like a true wilderness." Habitat includes impressive groves of old-growth sugar maple, white pine, and eastern hemlock. In 1998, Andres, along with two downstate Michigan bird experts, Mike and Susan Kielb, identified more than one hundred bird species along transects in various habitats in the second year of a three-year study.

"By continuing bird surveys in the central and western UP, I feel a strong bond to the land through knowing the species of birds that live here, by habitat and season," she says. "My persistence in this very seasonal survey of birds has provided me other private contracts from landowners setting up permanent conservation easements. Private landowners in the Keweenaw, as well as across the country, are becoming more conservation-minded. They want to know the diversity of wildlife on their lands and how to improve it. Bird surveys provide an excellent picture from year to year."

Michigan's forest products industry is noticing the work of people like Andres and others as well as conducting its own research. Companies are realizing that commercial forest-management practices can influence the reproductive success of birds as well as the long-term health of the trees. "Nearly ten years ago we started looking at how forest management impacts songbirds, with an emphasis on the neotropical birds because they're more sensitive to disturbances," says John Johnson, the technical service manager with Mead Corporation in Escanaba, Michigan. Mead, the largest landowner in Michigan, owns seven hundred thousand acres of forest in the UP. "Our corporate culture has changed," says Johnson, who has bachelor's and master's degrees in forest biology. "Today, forest management must encompass more resources— such as fisheries, wild-life, and aesthetics—than just wood fiber."

Since 1994, the Sustainable Forests Initiative, a movement led by the forest products industry, has mandated improved operating procedures for harvesting timber that could protect some habitat for birds. The initiative's goals include protecting water quality, enhancing wildlife habitat, supporting research, minimizing the visual impact of harvesting, and contributing to species biodiversity.

Mead supports the initiative, says Johnson, and has been forging relationships with biologists and researchers in the UP since 1988, including people who work with loons, eagles, and neotropical migrants. "In 1991, we began a serious neotropical-migrant research and training effort with Whitewater Associates scientists Dean Premo and Beth Rogers," says Johnson.

Robert Flasch, a Mead forester, recalls snowshoeing through a hardwood forest with Premo and Rogers that year. "They knew little about forestry," he says. "We didn't understand their basis for research." Three days later, each had gained a knowledge and understanding of the other's work, and today their relationship remains strong. "It has been a rich experience working with Whitewater Associates," says Flasch, who has lived in the UP for nearly a quarter century and has traversed its entire length and width. The data provided by this group of scientists gave Mead several opportunities to improve the diversity of flora and fauna in northern hardwood stands that they harvest. For example, in certain areas, Mead employees leave understory plants such as hemlock, white spruce, and cedar instead of clear-cutting. That way ground nesters such as ovenbirds can still breed in those forests. The corporation is avoiding harvesting timber from vernal ponds that attract not only birds, but also other rare creatures including salamanders and tiny frogs. These species need vernal ponds, small forest wetlands that dry in summer, for breeding. Early neotropical migrants depend upon vernal ponds because they are the first of the wetlands in the UP to thaw and produce the insects the birds need during their journey. "Vernal ponds are the hub of activity during migration," says Flasch. Hardwood leaves feed the vernal pond system by dropping in the fall and decaying. As they decay, they add nutrients needed by the creatures living in the pond. Mead leaves a hardwood buffer around vernal ponds to help maintain the ecosystem. Mead is also creating or leaving vegetative buffer zones between logging roads and forests to increase bird diversity.

Mead plants trees for later harvesting, and one of the most important of these is the red pine, a tree that provides softwood used in quality papermaking, something the company's customers demand, says Johnson. Red pine plantations, however, are not necessarily good habitat for birds and other creatures. Some scientists have called red pine plantations "biological deserts." But according to Johnson, research is showing that young stands of red pines do offer some breeding habitat for birds. "We don't have the definitive answers on the red pine plantations," says Johnson. "I'm not sure we've ended that debate yet."

Research on neotropical migrants is in its infancy. Much more needs to be learned, and many scientists are leading the way. Ray Rustem, the Natural Heritage Program supervisor for the Michigan DNR, is coordinating Michigan's participation in an international project called Partners in Flight, designed to identify why some populations of neotropical migrants are dwindling and what can be done to reverse the decline. The U.S. Forest Service, the U.S. Fish and Wildlife Service, state fish and wildlife agencies, the National Audubon Society, The Nature Conservancy, the Cornell Laboratory of Ornithology, universities, and forest-product industry personnel are working together on this project.

Susan Andres meanwhile has moved to Michigan's Lower Peninsula to pursue a full-time career. However, Andres knows she will one day return to the UP and that she will always consider it one of her homes.

"Once you survey an area, you never lose sight of a certain tree, much like you know where every flower is in your backyard," she says.

Andres offers hope that those who choose an uncommon existence in the UP will help preserve the avian creatures of a great wilderness. Listening to her, we believe that songs will run deep in the UP for centuries to come.

Pied-billed Grebe and chick

Epilogue

APRIL 25, MID-MORNING. "He's a feisty little guy," says a Whitefish Point Observatory bird bander, her middle finger and thumb wrapped snugly but not too tightly around a black-capped chickadee's neck as the bird nips at her hands.

"He has his own special band," the bander tells a six-year-old boy who is eagerly watching. "These pliers are designed especially for these little bands. They open up the tiny band that fits on his legs. See how little his feet are?" she says, snapping on the band.

"Whenever this guy goes anywhere and someone captures him again, they'll know he came from here," she tells the boy. "Now, we'll get a good measure of him. We'll measure from his shoulder to the end of his wing. It's about sixty-three millimeters. The tail is about fifty-nine millimeters.

"Birds have an area like our breastbone," she says, blowing gently on the chickadee's feathers to expose the fulcrum where fat is deposited. "See this yellowish part? It's all filled up with fat. This means he's been eating really well.

"We can't tell if it's a male or a female. But maybe someday when we have enough data, we will be able to tell. The last thing we do is weigh the bird."

She places the chickadee into a white bag with a red string. The chickadee weighs twelve and five-tenths grams. The bander strokes the head gently as she talks. "It seems to calm them down."

She then places the chickadee to the boy's ear. "Hear that thumping?" The sound is like Morse code—many times faster than the human heartbeat. Then, she gently places the chickadee in the boy's hand. "Hold out your hand and let it fly away," she says.

He does. The chickadee lands on a nearby branch, preens, then flies.

"That boy will remember that experience forever," says the bander. And the more people remember and understand, the more they are likely to interact positively with nature, perhaps to devote some of their life to studying birds, she says.

So while the current researchers work in Michigan's UP, the future researchers are right behind them. Perhaps one of them is a young child who heard the rapid beating of a chickadee's heart, and felt in his own heart a stirring to live with the birds.

The Birds of *Northern Flights*

Michigan's Upper Peninsula has hosted more than 300 bird species; birders have seen that many alone at Whitefish Point Bird Observatory. At least, and probably more than 200 of these birds breed in the UP. The following is a list of the bird species mentioned in this book.

Bittern, American	*Botaurus lentiginosus*
Bluebird, Eastern	*Sialia sialis*
Chickadee, Black-capped	*Poecile atricapillus*
Chickadee, Boreal	*Poecile hudsonicus*
Crane, Sandhill	*Grus canadensis*
Crossbill, Red	*Loxia curvirostra*
Crossbill, White-winged	*Loxia leucoptera*
Dove, Mourning	*Zenaida macroura*
Duck, Ring-necked	*Aythya collaris*
Eagle, Bald	*Haliaeetus leucocephalus*
Eagle, Golden	*Aquila chrysaetos*
Falcon, Peregrine	*Falco peregrinus*
Flicker, Northern	*Colaptes auratus*
Flycatcher, Least	*Empidonax minimus*
Flycatcher, Olive-sided	*Contopus borealis*
Flycatcher, Yellow-bellied	*Empidonax flaviventris*
Goldeneye, Common	*Bucephala clangula*
Goose, Canada	*Branta canadensis*
Goshawk, Northern	*Accipiter gentilis*
Grebe, Pied-billed	*Podilymbus podiceps*
Grosbeak, Evening	*Coccothraustes vespertinus*
Grosbeak, Rose-breasted	*Pheucticus ludovicianus*
Grouse, Ruffed	*Bonasa umbelius*
Grouse, Sharp-tailed	*Tympanuchus phasianellus*
Grouse, Spruce	*Dendragapus canadensis*

Gyrfalcon	*Falco rusticolus*
Harrier, Northern	*Circus cyaneus*
Hawk, Broad-winged	*Buteo platypterus*
Hawk, Cooper's	*Accipiter cooperii*
Hawk, Red-shouldered	*Buteo lineatus*
Hawk, Red-tailed	*Buteo jamaicensis*
Hawk, Rough-legged	*Buteo lagopus*
Hawk, Sharp-shinned	*Accipiter striatus*
Heron, Great Blue	*Ardea herodias*
Jay, Blue	*Cyanocitta cristata*
Jay, Gray	*Perisoreus canadensis*
Junco, Dark-eyed	*Junco hyemalis*
Kestrel, American	*Falco sparverius*
Kingbird, Eastern	*Tyrannus tyrannus*
Kinglet, Golden-crowned	*Regulus satrapa*
Loon, Common	*Gavia immer*
Loon, Pacific	*Gavia pacifica*
Loon, Red-throated	*Gavia stellata*
Merganser, Common	*Mergus merganser*
Merganser, Red-breasted	*Mergus serrator*
Merlin	*Falco columbarius*
Nuthatch, Red-breasted	*Sitta canadensis*
Oldsquaw	*Clangula hyemalis*
Osprey	*Pandion haliaetus*
Ovenbird	*Seiurus aurocapillus*
Owl, Barred	*Strix varia*
Owl, Boreal	*Aegolius funereus*
Owl, Great Gray	*Strix nebulosa*
Owl, Great Horned	*Bubo virginianus*
Owl, Long-eared	*Asio otus*
Owl, Northern Hawk-	*Surnia ulula*
Owl, Northern Saw-whet	*Aegolius acadicus*
Owl, Short-eared	*Asio flammeus*
Owl, Snowy	*Nyctea scandiaca*
Parula, Northern	*Parula americana*

Pewee, Eastern Wood-	*Contopus virens*
Pheasant, Ring-necked	*Phasianus colchicus*
Phoebe, Eastern	*Sayornis phoebe*
Pine Siskin	*Carduelis pinus*
Prairie-Chicken, Greater	*Tympanuchus cupido*
Rail, Yellow	*Coturnicops noveboracensis*
Raven, Common	*Corvus corax*
Redstart, American	*Setophaga ruticilla*
Robin, American	*Turdus migratorius*
Sapsucker, Yellow-bellied	*Sphyrapicus varius*
Scaup, Greater	*Aytha marila*
Scoter, White-winged	*Melanitta fusca*
Screech-owl, Eastern	*Otus asio*
Snipe, Common	*Gallinago gallinago*
Sparrow, Le Conte's	*Ammodramus leconteii*
Sparrow, Vesper	*Pooecetes gramineus*
Sparrow, White-throated	*Zonotrichia albicollis*
Swallow, Cliff	*Hirundo pyrrhonata*
Swallow, Tree	*Tachycineta bicolor*
Swan, Trumpeter	*Cygnus buccinator*
Swift, Chimney	*Chaetura pelagica*
Tanager, Scarlet	*Piranga olivacea*
Teal, Green-winged	*Anas crecca*
Tern, Black	*Chlidonias niger*
Tern, Forster's	*Sterna forsteri*
Thrush, Hermit	*Catharus guttatus*
Thrush, Swainson's	*Catharus ustulatus*
Veery	*Catharus fuscescens*
Vireo, Blue-headed (formerly Solitary Vireo)	*Vireo solitarius*
Vireo, Red-eyed	*Vireo olivaceus*
Vulture, Turkey	*Cathartes aura*
Warbler, Blackburnian	*Dendroica fusca*
Warbler, Black-throated Blue	*Dendroica caerulescens*
Warbler, Black-throated Green	*Dendroica virens*

Warbler, Chestnut-sided	*Dendroica pensylvanica*
Warbler, Kirtland's	*Dendroica kirtlandii*
Warbler, Mourning	*Oporornis philadelphia*
Warbler, Nashville	*Vermivora ruficapilla*
Warbler, Palm	*Dendroica palmarum*
Warbler, Yellow-rumped	*Dendroica coronata*
Waxwing, Cedar	*Bombycilla cedrorum*
Woodpecker, Black-backed	*Picoides arcticus*
Woodpecker, Downy	*Picoides pubescens*
Woodpecker, Pileated	*Dryocopus pileatus*
Wren, House	*Troglodytes aedon*
Wren, Marsh	*Cistothorus palustris*
Wren, Sedge	*Cistothorus platensis*
Wren, Winter	*Troglodytes troglodytes*

Resource List

To learn more about the birds and researchers of Michigan's Upper Peninsula, to find out about volunteer opportunities, or to make a donation, contact the following:

BioDiversity Research Institute
195 Main St.
Freeport, Maine 04032

Friends of the Porkies
P.O. Box 694
White Pine, Michigan 49971

Isle Royale National Park and
Isle Royale Natural History Association
800 E. Lakeshore Drive
Houghton, Michigan 49931-1895

Michigan Audubon Society
6011 West St. Joseph Hwy.
Suite 403
P.O. Box 80527
Lansing, Michigan 48908-0527

Michigan Department of Natural Resources
Crystal Falls Management Unit Office
1420 Highway US-2 West, Crystal Falls, Michigan 49920

> Baraga Field Office
> 427 US-41 North, Baraga, Michigan 49908

> Newberry Management Unit Office
> Route 4, Box 796
> Newberry, Michigan 49868

> Norway Field Office
> P.O. Box 126, Norway, Michigan 49870

Sault Ste. Marie Field Office
P.O. Box 798, Sault Ste. Marie, Michigan 49783

Michigan Nature Association
7981 Beard Road, Box 102
Avoca, Michigan 48006

Michigan Sharp-tailed Grouse Association
c/o Rick Baetsen
P.O. Box 623
Walloon Lake, Michigan 49796

The Nature Conservancy, Michigan Chapter
2840 E. Grand River Ave.
East Lansing, Michigan 48823

Nequaket Natural History Association
P.O. Box 103
White Pine, Michigan 49971

North American Loon Fund
6 Lily Pond Road
Gilford, New Hampshire 03246

Ottawa National Forest Headquarters
E6248 US Highway 2
Ironwood, Michigan 49938

   Ontonagon Ranger District
   1209 Rockland Road
   Ontonagon, Michigan 49953

   Watersmeet Ranger District
   Old US 2/P.O. Box 276
   Watersmeet, Michigan 49969

The Peregrine Fund
World Center for Birds of Prey
5666 West Flying Hawk Lane
Boise, Idaho 83709

Pictured Rocks National Lakeshore
National Park Service
U.S. Department of Interior
P.O. Box 40
Munising, Michigan 49862

Porcupine Mountains Wilderness State Park
c/o Robert Sprague
Michigan Department of Natural Resources
412 South Boundary Road
Ontonagon, Michigan 49963

The Ruffed Grouse Society
451 McCormick Road
Coraopolis, Pennsylvania 15108

Seney National Wildlife Refuge
HCR 2, Box 1
Seney, Michigan 49883

Whitefish Point Bird Observatory
NC 48, Box 115
Paradise, Michigan 49768

Bibliography

BOOKS

Ashworth, William. *The Late Great Lakes: An Environmental History.* New York: Alfred A. Knopf, Inc., 1986.

Barnes, Burton V., and Warren H. Wagner, Jr. *Michigan Trees.* Ann Arbor: University of Michigan Press, 1992.

Bent, Arthur Cleveland. *Life Histories of North American Gallinaceous Birds.* New York: Dover Publications, Inc., 1963.

Benyus, Janine M. *Northwoods Wildlife—Watcher's Guide to Habitats.* Minocqua, Wisconsin: NorthWord Press, Inc., 1989.

Brewer, Richard, Gail McPeek, and Raymond J. Adams, Jr. *The Atlas of Breeding Birds of Michigan.* East Lansing: Michigan State University Press, 1991.

Childress, Diana. *Prehistoric People of North America.* Broomhall, Pennsylvania: Chelsea House Publishers, 1997.

Dunne, Pete. *The Wind Masters: The Lives of North American Birds of Prey.* Boston: Houghton Mifflin Co., 1995.

Dunning, Joan. *The Loon: Voice of the Wilderness.* Boston: Houghton Mifflin Co., 1985.

Harrison, Hal H. *Wood Warblers' World.* New York: Simon and Schuster, Inc., 1984.

Johnsgard, Paul A. *North American Owls: Biology and Natural History.* Washington and London: Smithsonian Institution Press, 1988.

Kaufman, Kenn. *Advanced Birding.* Boston: Houghton Mifflin Co., 1990.

Kircher, John C. *Ecology of Eastern Forests.* Boston: Houghton Mifflin Co., 1988.

Littlejohn, Bruce, and Drew Wayland. *Superior: The Haunted Shore.* Buffalo, New York: Firefly Books, 1995.

Petrides, George A. *Eastern Trees.* Peterson Field Guide Series. Boston: Houghton Mifflin Co., 1988.

Rafferty, Michael, and Robert Sprague. *Porcupine Mountains Companion.* 3rd edition. White Pine, Michigan: Nequaket Natural History Associates, 1995.

Smith, Helen V. *Michigan Wildflowers.* Bloomfield Hills, Michigan: Cranbrook Institute of Science, 1966.

MAGAZINE ARTICLES

Baetsen, Rick. "Hooked on Sharptails." *Michigan Out-of-Doors,* May 1991.

———. "Michigan's Courting Grouse." *The Torch Magazine,* Winter 1986.

Caron, Jamson, Jr. "Spring Migration at Whitefish Point." *Michigan Out-of-Doors,* May 1993.

De Vore, Sheryl. "Dabbling Diver." *Wildfowl Carving And Collecting,* Fall 1992.

———. "Songbirds of the Illinois Forest." *The Nature of Illinois* 2, no. 4 (Spring 1995).

———. "Wild Cards." *American Birds,* Fall 1993.

Dickson, Tom. "Shadow over Sharptails." *The Minnesota Volunteer,* March–April 1993.

Donarski, Dan. "Sharp-tailed Grouse of Chippewa County." *Michigan Outdoor Journal,* September 1993.

McIntyre, Judith W., and Michael S. Quinton. "The Common Loon Cries for Help." *National Geographic,* April 1989.

"Migratory Songbirds Benefit from Efforts on Both Sides of the Border." *The Conservator* (The Nature Conservancy Illinois Chapter News), Summer 1994.

Niergarth, Grover. "Whitefish Point Bird Observatory: An Education Research Station." *The Michigan Audubon News* 35, no. 2.

Paton, Jim. "Great Lakes Birding: Whitefish Point, Michigan." *Birding* 30, no. 6 (December 1988).

St. John, Paige. "Yodelers of the North." *American Birds,* summer 1993.

"Sharptails' Plight Slotted for New Recognition." *The Northwoods Call,* February 1996.

Tozer, Ron, and Ron Pittaway. "Finding the Phantom Spruce Grouse." *Ontario Birds* 8, no. 2 (1990).

TECHNICAL PUBLICATIONS

Amman, G. A. *The Prairie Grouse of Michigan.* Lansing: Michigan Department of Conservation, 1957.

Andres, Sue. *Monitoring Neotropical Breeding Birds on the Ottawa National Forest 1995: Effects of Management on Habitat Quality.* East Lansing: Michigan Birds and Natural History 3, no. 3 (1996).

Bart, Jonathan. "Survey Methods for Breeding Yellow Rails." *Journal of Wildlife Management* 48, no. 4 (1984).

Baumgartner, John E. and Alice H. Kell[e]y [*sic*]. "Summary of the Whitefish Point Bird Observatory Annual Report for 1979." *The Jack-Pine Warbler* 59, no. 2 (1982).

Bookhout, Theodore A. *Report of a Survey of Breeding Yellow Rails on Seney NWR, 1991.* Ohio Cooperative Fish and Wildlife Research Unit, Columbus, Ohio: Ohio State University, 1991.

Bookhout, Theodore A. "Yellow Rail." In *The Birds of North America,* No.139, eds. A. Poole and F. Gill. Philadelphia: The Academy of Natural Sciences; Washington, D.C.: The American Ornithologists' Union, 1995.

Bull, E. L. and J. R. Duncan. "Great Gray Owl *(Strix nebulosa)."* In *The Birds of North America,* No.41, eds. A. Poole and F. Gill. Philadelphia: The Academy of Natural Sciences; Washington, D.C.: The American Ornithologists' Union, 1993.

Devereux, James, Thomas Carpenter, and Katherine Durham. "Spring Migration Pattern of Sharp-Shinned Hawks Passing Whitefish Point, Michigan." *Journal of Field Ornithology* 56, no. 4 (1985).

Doepker, Robert V., Richard D. Earle, and John J. Ozoga. "Characteristics of Blackburnian Warbler: *(Dendroica fuxca),* Breeding Habitat in Upper Michigan." *The Canadian Field Naturalist* 106 (1992).

Duncan, J. R., and P. A. Duncan. "Northern Hawk Owl *(Surnia ulula)."* In *The Birds of North America,* No.356, eds. A. Poole and F. Gill. Philadelphia: The Academy of Natural Sciences; Washington, D.C.: The American Ornithologists' Union, 1998.

Evers, David C. *Northern Great Lakes Common Loon Monitoring Program: 1992 and 1993 Field Season Final Reports.* Paradise, Michigan: Whitefish Point Bird Observatory, 1994.

Hayward, G. D., and P. H. Hayward. "Boreal Owl *(Aegolius funereus)*." In *The Birds of North America,* No.63, eds. A. Poole and F. Gill. Philadelphia: The Academy of Natural Sciences; Washington, D.C.: The American Ornithologists' Union, 1993.

Holt, D. W., and S. M. Leasure. "Short-eared Owl *(Asio flammeus)*" In *The Birds of North America,* No.62, eds. A. Poole and F. Gill. Philadelphia: The Academy of Natural Sciences; Washington, D.C.: The American Ornithologists' Union, 1993.

Kelley, Alice H. "Spring Migration at Whitefish Point, 1966-1967." *The Jack-Pine Warbler* 50, no. 3 (1973).

Kelley, Alice H. and J. O. L. Roberts. "Spring Migration of Owls at Whitefish Point." *The Jack-Pine Warbler* 49, no. 3 (1972).

Kenner, Brian C. *Peregrine Falcon Re-establishment Efforts.* Pictured Rocks Resource Report. Munising, Michigan: National Park Service, 1992.

McIntyre, J.W., and J.F. Barr. "Common Loon *(Gavia immer)*." In *The Birds of North America,* No.3130A, eds. A. Poole and F. Gill. Philadelphia: The Academy of Natural Sciences; Washington, D.C.: The American Ornithologists' Union, 1997.

Michigan DNR Nongame Program, Ottawa National Forest. *The Bergland Release of the Peregrine Falcon in Michigan's Upper Peninsula.* Ironwood, Michigan, 1988.

Stenzel, Jeffrey R. "Ecology of Breeding Yellow Rails at Seney National Wildlife Refuge." Thesis, Ohio State University, 1982.

United States Department of Agriculture, Forest Service, Northeastern Area. *Forest Health Assessment for the Northeastern Area,* Washington, D.C., 1993.

Wood, Norman A. *Results of the Shiras Expeditions to Whitefish Point, Michigan—Birds.* Sixteenth Report. Lansing: Michigan Academy of Science, [1915].

PAMPHLETS, NEWSLETTERS, AND OTHER JOURNALS AND PUBLICATIONS

Gullion, Gordon W. *The Ruffed Grouse.* Coraopolis, Pennsylvania: The Ruffed Grouse Society, 1990.

National Park Service, Pictured Rocks National Lakeshore. *Day Hikes in the Grand Marais Area.* Munising, Michigan: National Park Service, 1993.

Reflections on Paradise. Paradise, Michigan: Paradise Press, 1989.

Spruce Grouse Society. *Fool-Hens Forever.* vol. 2. Spruce Grouse Society, 1995.

Whitefish Point Bird Observatory. *The Migrant,* vol. 9–12. Paradise, Michigan: Whitefish Point Bird Observatory, 1989–1992.

Sheryl De Vore —Courtesy of the Lake County Forest Preserves

About the Author

Sheryl De Vore is a naturalist, editor, and award-winning environmental writer. A graduate of Northern Illinois University with a writing certificate from Northwestern University, De Vore contributes to *Birder's World*, *WildBird*, and *Chicago Wilderness* magazines. Her many honors include journalist of the year from Pioneer Press Newspapers, an award for excellence in environmental reporting from the Chicago Audubon Society, and best environmental writing from the Suburban Newspapers of America. De Vore is the assistant managing editor for Pioneer Press and the chief editor for *Meadowlark*, a journal published by the Illinois Ornithological Society. She lives in Mundelein, Illinois.

About the Illustrator

Denis Kania is art editor for the Illinois Ornithological Society and a teacher in the naturalist certification program at the Morton Arboretum. Kania has exhibited his work in more than a dozen states and has created commissioned artwork for The Nature Conservancy of Illinois and other organizations. He lives in Naperville, Illinois.

We encourage you to patronize your local bookstores. Most stores will order any title that they do not stock. You may also order directly from Mountain Press by mail, using the order form provided below, or by calling our toll-free number and using your Visa or MasterCard. We will gladly send you a complete catalog upon request.

Some other titles of interest:

____An Introduction to Northern California Birds	$14.00
____An Introduction to Southern California Birds	$14.00
____Birds of the Central Rockies	$14.00
____Birds of the Pacific Northwest Mountains	$14.00
____Edible and Medicinal Plants of the West	$21.00
____A Field Guide to Nearby Nature	$15.00
____Hollows, Peepers, and Highlanders An Appalachian Mountain Ecololgy	$14.00
____OWLS Whoo are they?	$12.00
____Roadside Geology of Indiana	$18.00
____Watchable Birds of California	$18.00
____Watchable Birds of the Great Basin	$16.00
____Watchable Birds of the Rocky Mountains	$14.00
____Watchable Birds of the Southwest	$14.00

Please include $3.00 per order to cover shipping and handling. Send the books marked above. I enclose $_____

Name_____

Address_____

City/State/Zip_____

☐ Payment enclosed (check or money order in U.S. funds)

Bill my: ☐ VISA ☐ MasterCard Expiration Date:_____

Card No._____

Signature _____

MOUNTAIN PRESS PUBLISHING COMPANY
P. O. Box 2399 • Missoula, MT 59806
Order Toll Free 1-800-234-5308 • Have your Visa or MasterCard ready.
e-mail: mtnpress@montana.com • website: www.mtnpress.com